Edward Leete

The family of William Leete, one of the first settlers of Guilford

Edward Leete

The family of William Leete, one of the first settlers of Guilford

ISBN/EAN: 9783337152451

Printed in Europe, USA, Canada, Australia, Japan

Cover: Foto ©ninafisch / pixelio.de

More available books at **www.hansebooks.com**

OF

WILLIAM LEETE,

ONE OF THE

FIRST SETTLERS OF GUILFORD, CONN.,

AND

GOVERNOR OF NEW HAVEN AND CONNECTICUT
COLONIES.

Compiled by EDWARD L. LEETE,
Guilford, Conn.

NEW HAVEN:
TUTTLE, MOREHOUSE & TAYLOR, PRINTERS.
1884.

NOTE.

DEA. EDWARD L. LEETE, the compiler of this work, when he had brought it near to completion, passed away by death; and the undersigned has been requested to supervise the work as it passes through the press, also making some additions and adding a few notes.

ALVAN TALCOTT.

GUILFORD, CONN., May 31, 1884.

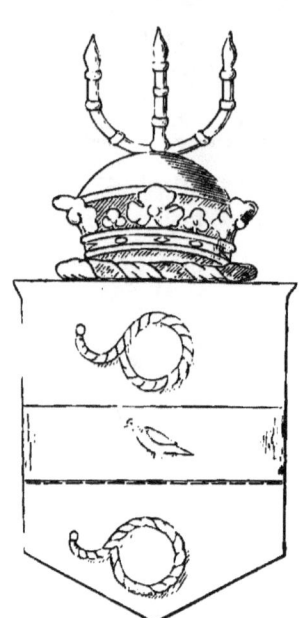

INTRODUCTION.

LITTLE was known in this country respecting the antecedents of the Leete family (descendants of Wm. Leete) in America, until the reception here, quite recently, of an interesting volume, entitled "The Family of Leete." This book was printed in London, in 1881, "for private circulation," and was generously sent to public libraries in this country by Joseph Leete, Esq., of Eversden, South Norwood Park, S. E. Surrey, England. To this book we are indebted for most that we know of the family history anterior to the emigration of Wm. Leete to this country in 1639.

From it we learn the great antiquity of the family name; that Gerard Letie or Lete held lands in Morden, Cambridgeshire, in 1209, in the reign of King John; that Matthew Lety held lands in 1370; that Bobertus fil Lete was assessed to a subsidy in 1326-27; that John Leet, grocer, of London, made a will which was proved in 1442; that John Lete, of Cottenham, made a will proved in 1523; that Henry Lette, of Cottenham, husbandman, made a will proved in 1527; that Henry Leete, of Comberton, made a will proved in 1541, etc.

From the same source comes our knowledge of the Leete coat of arms, for though used by Governor Leete in this country, as his seal proves, all knowledge of its use, and even of its existence, had long been obliterated. It is described as follows: Argent, on a fesse, gules, between two rolls of matches, sable, fired proper, a martlet, or. Crest: on a ducal coronet, or, an antique lamp, or, fired proper. The origin and signification of the arms have not been ascertained.

The name anciently was variously spelled—Letie, Lete, Lety, Leet, Lette, Lytte, Leete, etc., etc. As early however as the reign of Queen Elizabeth, three hundred years ago, Thomas Leete, of Ockington, spelled his name *Leete*, and his descendants, for two hundred years, with great unanimity, followed that spelling of the name, and it is the common spelling still. Latterly, however, some branches of the family write the name *Leet*, omitting the final *e*. In this book it is uniformly retained, but it should not be forgotten that some important families *now* spell the name without it.

Wm. Leete was born in Dodington, Huntingdonshire, England, in 1612 or 1613. His grandfather was Thomas Leete, of Ockington, Cambridgeshire, England, who married Maria Slade, of Rushton, Northamptonshire, daughter of Edward Slade. Thomas Leete had four children, two sons and two daughters. Both his sons he named *John*. These were distinguished, in speaking of them, by their place of residence, John of Dodington (the elder), and John of Islington. His daughters were Jane and Rebecca. Jane married Richard Dale and Rebecca married Thomas Fowler.

John Leete of Dodington, son of Thomas of Ockington, married Anna Shute, daughter of Robert Shute, one of the Justices of the King's Bench. They had two sons, William, who came to Guilford and was afterward Governor Leete, and John, of Midlow Grange, Huntingdonshire, and a daughter Anne, who married Robert Raby.

William Leete, son of John of Dodington, "was bred to the law, and served for a considerable time as clerk in the Bishop's Court at Cambridge, where, observing the oppressions and cruelties then practiced on the conscientious and virtuous Puritans, he was led to examine more thoroughly their doctrines and practice, and eventually to become a Puritan himself and to give up his office."

He came to America in Rev. Mr. Whitfield's company, and was one of the signers of the Plantation Covenant on shipboard, June 1, 1639, arriving in New Haven about July 10. When they had agreed upon Guilford as a place to settle, he was one of six selected to purchase the land of the native Indians, in trust, for the plantation until their organization.

[When the lands in the village were surveyed and laid out for individual ownership, he selected for his residence a lot opposite to that of William Chittenden, on the corner of what are now Broad and River streets, a site overlooking Menunketuck river as it winds its way through meadows reclaimed from the sea, as green then as now, or, when it meets a full tide, expanding into a broad lake. His outlying lands (about 250 acres) were located chiefly some three miles away, in the southwesterly quarter of the town, and the place was named from him Leete's Island. That which goes by this name is not strictly an island, but a part of these lands, at first called Horse Island, is surrounded with salt meadows, and of course was once an island.

This section of Guilford still retains the name of Leete's Island, and the lands have been owned and occupied by Leetes almost exclusively down to the present generation. It has now its post office and store, and has recently come into prominent notice as the location of Beattie's stone quarries.

The following is a fac-simile of Governor Leete's signature :

[signature: William Leete]

His seal has been preserved in the family to the present time. It bears a correct representation of the Leete Coat of Arms.]   T.

Mr. Leete was called upon to fill many public offices. He was clerk of the plantation from 1639 to 1662. He was one of four to whom was entrusted the whole civil power of the plantation, without limitation, until a church was formed, June 19 (June 29 N. S.), 1643. When the church was formed, he was selected as one of the seven pillars "for the foundation work." Samuel Disborough and William Leete were chosen to meet the court at New Haven in 1643, when the combination of the jurisdiction of the New Haven Colony was planned and organized, and Guilford, Milford, Stamford and other plantations, hitherto independent colonies, united in one jurisdiction with New Haven, establishing a General Court for the whole jurisdiction, to sit twice a year at New Haven in April and October, and to consist of the governor, deputy governor, and all the magistrates within the jurisdiction, and two deputies for every plantation. Mr. Leete was a deputy from Guilford to this court till 1650, and from 1651 to 1658 was the magistrate of the town. In 1658 he was chosen deputy governor of the colony, and continued in that office until 1661 when he was elected governor, which office he held until the union with Connecticut in 1664. After the union he was an assistant until 1669 when he was elected deputy governor of the Connecticut Colony, holding this office until 1676 when he was chosen governor, which position he retained by continuous reëlection until his death in 1683. Upon being elected governor he removed to Hartford, and being continued in office he remained there until his death, and was buried there.

In Treasurer John Talcott's Account Book, now in the State Library in Hartford, under date of April 18, 1683, is this charge to Connecticut Colony :

"To 11 pound of powder for the Great Guns at Gou leet's funerall, lb 01 : 07 : 06."

His tombstone was discovered about 1830, in the ancient burial ground in the rear of the First Church of Hartford, where it had long been hidden by an accumulation of earth. His descendants of the present generation have erected a plain granite monument to his memory.

"During the term of forty years," says Dr. Trumbull, the historian, "he was Magistrate, Deputy Governor, or Governor of one or other of the colonies. In both colonies he presided in times of the greatest difficulty, yet always conducted himself with such integrity and wisdom as to meet the public approbation."

When two of the Judges of King Charles I., Goffe and Whalley, fled to New England for safety, upon the restoration of Charles II. to the throne of his father, Mr. Leete exerted himself for their protection. For several days they were secreted in the cellar of his store and fed from his table. And at other times and in other ways he rendered them important aid. The cellar where the Judges were concealed is still to be seen in much the same condition as when they occupied it.

The object of these pages is to give, as far as possible, a record of the descendants of Governor Leete, by families, in genealogical order down to the present time, in the case of all that bear the Leete name. In the case of descendants of other names the record will not be continued after the first generation in each case. Our record for the first hundred years after the settlement of Guilford is nearly complete. No Leete moved out of the town in more than ninety years from its first settlement, and the town records furnish material for the family record. Moreover, a large portion of the family has always remained in the town or vicinity. Of the present inhabitants of the town more than eighty are Leetes. The record of these has been mostly preserved, and through them the record, partial or complete, of many who have moved away has been ascertained. Nevertheless in the removals and re-removals of the last one hundred and fifty years, branches of the family have, from time to time, been lost sight of, and consequently many names which properly belong on these pages are not found here.

LEETE GENEALOGY.

1

Gov. Wm. Leete, son of John Leete, of Dodington, England, married 1st, in England, about 1638, Anne Payne, daughter of Rev. John Payne, of Southhoe. She was the mother of all his children and died Sept. 1, 1668. He m. 2d, Apr. 7, 1670, Sarah, widow of Henry Rutherford. She died Feb. 10, 1673. He m. 3d, Mary, widow 1st of Gov. Francis Newman, and 2d of Rev. Nicholas Street. She died Dec. 13, 1683. He died Apr. 16, 1683.

CHILDREN.

2. John,   b.   1639, m. Mary Chittenden.
3. Andrew,   1643, m. Elizabeth Jordan.
4. William,   m. Mary Fenn.
5. Abigail,   m. Rev. J. Woodbridge.
6. Caleb,   Aug. 24, 1651, d. Jan. 13, 1673.
7. Gratiana,   Dec. 22, 1653, s. Imbecile and lame.
8. Peregrine, Jan. 12, 1658, d. young.
9. Joshua,   1659, d. Feb. 22, 1660.
10. Anna,   Mar. 10, 1661, m. John Trowbridge.

2

John Leete, son of Gov. Wm., m. Oct. 4, 1670, Mary Chittenden, dau. of Wm. Chittenden and Joanna Sheafe of Guilford, born in 1647. He is said to have been the first white child born in Guilford. He died Nov. 25, 1692, aged 53. She died March 9, 1712, aged 65.

11. Ann,   b. Aug. 5, 1671, m. John Collins.
12. John,   Jan. 4, 1674, m. Sarah Allen.
13. Joshua,   July 7, 1676, m. Mary Munger.
14. Sarah,   Dec. 16, 1677, m. Eliakim Marshall.
15. Pelatiah,   Mar. 26, 1681, m. Abigail Fowler.
16. Mehitabel,   Dec. 10, 1683, m. Dr. Anthony Labore.
17. Benjamin,   Dec. 26, 1686, m. Rachel Champion.
18. Daniel,   Sept. 23, 1689, d. y.

3

Hon. Andrew Leete, son of Gov. Wm., m. June 1, 1669, Elizabeth Jordan, dau. of Thomas and Dorothy Jordan. He succeeded in a good degree to the position of his father, in managing the affairs of the town and to some extent of the Colony. In 1677 he was elected to the honorable office of Assistant in the Connecticut Colony, and was annually re-elected till his death. It was while holding this office that he became principally instrumental in secreting and preserving the charter of the Colony during the usurpation of the government by Major Andross. For a season the charter was kept in his house at Guilford. His residence was on the northwest corner of Guilford Green, on what is now the Tuttle Place. He died aged 59, Oct. 31, 1702. His wife died March 4, 1701.

19. William,   b. Mar. 24, 1671, m. Hannah Stone.
20. Caleb,   Dec. 10, 1673, m. Mary Hubbard.
21. Samuel,   1677, m. Hannah Graves.
22. Dorothy,   1680, m. John Hopson.
23. Abigail,   1683, m. Abraham Bradley.
24. Mercy,   1688, m. Samuel Hooker.

8

William Leete, son of Gov. Wm., m. Mary Fenn, dau. of Benjamin Fenn, of Milford, Conn. He was a Deputy from Guilford to the "General Court" nearly every year while his father was governor of the Colony. He died June 1, 1687, and his widow m. 2d, Stephen Bradley, of Guilford. She died, aged 54, June 20, 1701.

 25. Mary, b. Jan. 11, 1672, m. Judge James Hooker.

5   *Woodbridge*

Abigail Leete, dau. of Gov. Wm., m. Oct. 26, 1671, Rev. John Woodbridge, of Killingworth, Conn., a graduate of Harvard, 1664. He died in 1690. She died Feb. 9, 1711.

 Rev. John, of West Springfield, Mass.
 Rev. Thomas Dudley, of Simsbury.
 Rev. Ephraim, of Groton, Conn.
 Mercy, m. Rev. Benj. Ruggles.

10   *Trowbridge*

Anna Leete, dau. of Gov. Wm., m. Nov. 19, 1682, John Trowbridge, born Nov. 23, 1661. He died at sea, June 30, 1689, aged 28. His widow m. 2d, May 9, 1696, Ebenezer Collins. She died, aged 86, Aug. 2, 1747.

 John, b. Nov. — 1684, m. Rebecca Elliot. [1705.
 Ann,   July 20, 1688, m. Rev. Sam'l Cook, Y. C.,

11   *Collins*

Ann Leete, dau. of John (2), m. July 23, 1691, John Collins, of Guilford, son of John Collins and Mary Trowbridge, born in 1665. She died, aged 53, Nov. 2, 1724. He died, aged 86, Jan. 24, 1751.

Ann,	b. May 9, 1692, m. Daniel Bartlett.
Mary,	April 11, 1694, s. d. Feb. 2, 1729.
John,	Feb. 23, 1696, m. Rachel Mix.
Timothy,	Feb. 11, 1698, d. Feb. 19, 1699. [Hyde.
Rev. Timothy.	April 13, 1699, Y. C., 1718, m. Elizabeth
Daniel,	June 13, 1701, m. Lois Cornwall.
Susannah,	Sept. 25, 1703, d. Oct. 5, 1703.
Samuel,	Nov. 2, 1704, m. Margery Leete (50).
Mercy,	Jan. 19, 1707, m. Samuel Hopson.
Oliver,	Oct. 18, 1710, m. Elizabeth Hall.
Avis,	April 1, 1714, m. Peter Buell.

12

John Leete, son of John (2), m. 1st, Sarah Allen, who died aged 36, Mar. 8, 1712. He m. 2d, Mehitabel Allis, by whom he had one child. He died aged 56, May, 1730.

26. John,	b. Jan.	2, 1699, m. Elizabeth Baldwin.
27. Mary,	Feb.	28, 1701, m. Abiel Elliot.
28. Gideon,	Feb.	4, 1703, m. Abigail Rossiter.
29. Sarah,	Aug.	28, 1705,
30. Reuben,	May	29, 1714, m. Lucy Bartlett.

13

Joshua Leete, son of John (2), m. June 21, 1709, Mary Munger, dau. of John Munger and Mary Evarts, of Guilford, born Aug. 19, 1689. She died, aged 32, Mar. 18, 1722. He m. 2d, Mar. 6, 1723, Mercy Eggleston, of Middletown, dau. of Samuel Eggleston, and widow of John Benton, of Guilford, born July 27, 1679. He died, aged 65, Apr. 24, 1742.

31. Jerusha, b. Nov. 14, 1711, m. John Shelley.

Joshua Leete became lost in the woods at Stony Creek, April 21, 1742, and was found dead in a swamp Apr. 24.

14

Sarah Leete, dau. of John (2), m. Aug. 23, 1704, Eliakim Marshall, of Windsor, Conn., son of Samuel Marshall and Mary Wilton, born July 10, 1669.

Dorothy, b.	Oct. 1, 1705,
Sarah,	June 27, 1709, d. y.
Sarah,	Jan. 29, 1711,
Mary,	Mar. 14, 1715,
Eliakim,	July 15, 1720, m. Sarah Hodge.

15

Dea. Pelatiah Leete, son of John (2), m. July 1, 1705, Abigail Fowler, dau. of Abraham Fowler and Elizabeth Bartlett, of Guilford, born in 1679, and soon after removed to Leete's Island, where no settlement had before been made. He built his house where Edward L. Leete recently lived and resided there the remainder of his life. He was a large landholder and a successful farmer. He kept a hundred head of neat cattle, and considered a hundred bushels of shelled corn to the acre no more than an average yield. The land upon which he settled he inherited. It was allotted to his grandfather, Gov. Leete, in 1660, became the portion of his father, John Leete, from whom it came to him. It is still owned by his descendants. He was a deacon in the Fourth Church of Guilford, and although chiefly engaged in private affairs was often elected to represent the town in the "General Court." He died, aged 87, Oct. 13, 1768. She died, aged 90, Oct. 22, 1769. They had lived together 63 years.

32. Abigail,	b. Sept. 13, 1707, s. d. June 2, 1792.	
33. Daniel,	Oct. 14, 1709, m. Rhoda Stone.	
34. Mehitabel,	Sept. 28, 1711, d. Oct. 21, 1711.	
35. Pelatiah,	Mar. 7, 1713, m. Lydia Cruttenden.	
36 Mehitabel,	1714, m. John Brewster.	

16 *Labore*

Mehitabel Leete, dau. of John (2). m. Jan. 4, 1711, Dr. Anthony Labore, a physician practicing his profession in Guilford, who came from Stratford. They had one child, Mehitabel, born Nov. 30, 1711, and died Jan. 5, 1714. Dr. Labore died Mar. 19, 1712. She m. 2d, Richard Blackleach, Jr., of Stratford.

17

Benjamin Leete, son of John (2), m. Oct. 26, 1714, Rachel Champion, of Lyme, dau. of Henry Champion, born Dec. 1, 1697. He was a tailor, and removed to Durham, Ct., in 1731, and died, aged 55, in 1741. She m. 2d, Mar. 22, 1750, Samuel Betts.

    37. Rachel, b. 1715.
    38. Benjamin, Apr. 8, 1717.
    39. Susannah, Mar. 19, 1719.
    40. Daniel, Jan. 16, 1721, m. Mehitabel Saville.
    41. Ezekiel, June 30, 1724.
    42. ⎰ Asa, July 21, 1726, m. Hannah Raynor.
    43. ⎱ Tamar, July 21, 1726,
    44. Temperance, Feb. 26, 1729.
    45. Levi, Mar. 3, 1731, m. Lydia Hotchkin.
    46. Sarah, Nov. 13, 1734, m. Stephen Leete (75).
    47. Leah, Mar. 7, 1740, m. Edward Benton.

19

William Leete, son of Andrew (3), m. Feb. 12, 1699, Hannah Stone, dau. of Wm. Stone, of Guilford, and Hannah Woulfe, born July 27, 1678. Wm. Leete died Jan. 26, 1736, aged 65.

48. Ann,   b. Mar. 6, 1700, m. Samuel Hopson.
49. Elizabeth,   Oct. 26, 1702, s. d. Sept. 17, 1769.
50. Margery,   Oct. 8, 1705, m. Samuel Collins.
51. Roland,   Aug. 6, 1708, m. Mercy Dudley.
52. William,   Dec. 12, 1711, Y.C. 1733, s.d. Sept. 21, 1756.
53. Jordan,   Oct.   1720, m. Rebecca Watrous.
54. Solomon,   Sept.   1722, m. Zipporah Stone.

20

Caleb Leete, son of Andrew (3), m. Nov. 4, 1697, Mary Hubbard, dau. of Daniel Hubbard and Elizabeth Jordan, of Guilford, born Feb. 16, 1676. She died, aged 43, April 22, 1719. He m. 2d, May 10, 1721, Abigail Cadwell (widow of Matthew Cadwell, of Hartford), who died Nov. 10, 1755. He died Dec. 3, 1760, aged 87.

He had been for twenty-five sessions a member of the "General Court."

55. Andrew,   b. June 1, 1700, d. y.
56. Caleb,   Nov. 19, 1702, d. Jan. 28, 1703.
57. Mary,   June 17, 1705, s. d. June 29, 1772.
58. Caleb,   Nov. 9, 1708, s. d. Dec. 15, 1752.
59. Rachel,   Mar. 31, 1710, d. June 14, 1710.
60. Dorothy,   Aug. 2, 1712, m. David Hurd.
61. Mercy,   1714, m. Jonathan Hubbard.
62. Rachel,   Jan. 30, 1718, m. Seth Stone.

21

Samuel Leete, son of Andrew (3), m. Nov. 28, 1723, Hannah Graves, dau. of Joseph and Margaret Graves, of Guilford, born Oct. 30, 1699. She died, aged 70, Mar. 26, 1770. He died, aged 74, Feb. 20, 1751.

63. Sybil, b. Oct. 18, 1724, m. Ebenezer Stone.
64. Samuel, June 25, 1726, m. Jane McNemor.
65. Anna, July 25, 1728, s. d. Oct 11, 1779.
66. Andrew, Nov. 6, 1731, m. Esther Blatchley.
67. Jared, Jan. 28, 1736, m. Hannah Hand.
68. Lucy, bap. Aug. 21, 1743, m. Samuel Barker.

22

Dorothy Leete, dau. of Andrew (3), m. Feb. 25, 1706, as 2d wife, John Hopson, of Guilford, son of Sergt. John Hopson, born Mar. 26, 1665. She had no children. He died, aged 65, Jan. 12, 1730.

23 *Stone*

Abigail Leete, dau. of Andrew (3), m. as 2d wife, Abraham Bradley, of Guilford. He died Apr. 20, 1721, aged 47. She m. 2d, as 2d wife, about 1725, Ebenezer Stone, son of Lieut. Nathaniel Stone, of Guilford, born Aug. 21, 1676. He died, aged 85, Aug. 18, 1761. She died, aged 84, Apr. 16, 1767. Child by last mar.

Abigail, b. Oct. 2, 1726, d. Nov. 23, 1783.

24 *Hooker*

Mercy Leete, dau. of Andrew (3), m. Jan. 9, 1711, Samuel Hooker, of Farmington, son of Samuel Hooker and Mehitabel Hamlin, born April 6, 1688. She died Feb. 4, 1751. He died, aged 99, March 1, 1787.

Andrew, b. Mar. 4, 1713.
Elizabeth, May 10, 1714.
Mercy, Oct. 22, 1719.
Mehitabel, May 15, 1722.
Sybil, May 19, 1724.
Samuel, Sept. 2, 1726.
Anne, Aug. 27, 1728.
Esther, July 30, 1731.
Thomas, Aug. 16, 1734.

25   *Hooker*

Mary Leete, dau. of Wm. (4), m. Aug. 1, 1691, Judge James Hooker, of Farmington, Conn., son of Rev. Samuel Hooker and Mary Willett, of Farmington, born Oct. 27, 1666. He resided in Guilford, and died, aged 76, Mar. 12, 1743. His widow died, aged 79, Oct. 5, 1752. Mr. Hooker was the first Judge of the Court of Probate for the District of Guilford, and a Magistrate.

    Mary,   b. Nov. 5, 1693, m. Rev. John Hart.
    Ann,   Jan. 26, 1695, m. Thomas Smith.
    Sarah,   Feb. 26, 1696, m. John Bartlett.
    Sir William, Oct. 16, 1702, s. d. Mar. 20, 1724.
    Mehitabel, May 10, 1704, m. John Smith.

26

John Leete, son of John (12), m. May 13, 1723, Elizabeth Baldwin, of Durham, Conn. They resided in Durham, where he died, aged 44, June, 1743.

    69. Elias,   b. April 30, 1724.
    70. Anna,   Feb. 13, 1726.
    71. John,   1727.
    72. David, bap. April 21, 1728.
    73. Chloe,   Jan. 25, 1730, m. Jeremiah Ranney.
    74. Phyllis,   Oct. 24, 1731.
    75. Stephen,   m. Sarah L. McKeen.
    76. Submit,   Jan. 8, 1738, m. Gershom Goodrich.
    76½. Hannah, Oct. 28, 1739.

27   *Elliot*

Mary Leete, dau. of John (12), m. in 1726, Abiel Elliot, son of Rev. Joseph Elliot and Mary Wyllis, born in 1692. Mr. Elliot died, aged 84, Oct. 28, 1776. His widow died, aged 79, Jan. 13, 1780.

Nathaniel, b. Aug. 15. 1728, m. Beulah Parmelee.
Wyllis, Feb. 9, 1731, m. Abigail Hull.
Rebecca, Sept. 8, 1733, m. Nathaniel Graves.
Timothy, Oct. 23, 1736, m. Rebecca Rose.
Levi, Nov. 1, 1739. s. d. Mar. 2, 1766.
Margery, Mar. 19, 1742, m. Theophilus Merriman.

Abiel Eliot and Mary Leete were great grandparents of Fitz-Greene Halleck, the poet. Their son Nathaniel's daughter, Mary, who m. Israel Halleck, was mother of the poet.

28

Gideon Leete, son of John (12), m. Sept. 6, 1727, Abigail Rossiter, widow of Timothy Rossiter, née Penfield. After her death he m. 2d, Catharine Strong, widow of Bryan Rossiter.

77. Allen, b. Oct. 20, 1728, m. Abigail Kelsey.
78. Gideon, May 5, 1731, m. Ann Parmelee.

Gideon Leete removed to Durham, Conn., and in 1745 to Chester, in the town of Saybrook. He died in 1781.

30

Reuben Leete, son of John (12), m. Lucy Bartlett, dau. of Timothy Bartlett and Susannah Cruttenden, of Guilford, born Jan. 11, 1729. They removed to Genesee, and he died, aged 80, Jan. 18, 1794. She died, aged 74, June, 1803.

79. John, b. m. Alpha Mann.
80. Reuben, 1764, d. Oct. 30, 1794.
81. Lucy, 1753, m. Johnson Bishop.
82. Ruth, m. Daniel P. Handy.
83. Sarah, m. —— Whitney.

Reuben, No. 80, was killed by a falling tree; a brother of his had been killed in 1767, by falling from a cart, æ. 16.

Shelley

31

Jerusha Leete, dau. of Joshua (13). m. Jan. 16, 1731, John Shelley, of Guilford, son of Shubael Shelley and widow Mary Evarts, of Guilford, born Feb. 4, 1710. He died, aged 41, Oct. 21, 1751. She died, aged 51, July 8, 1763.

Shubael, b.	1732, m. wd. Abigail Rice.
Mary,	Dec. 21, 1734, m. Eber Hall.
Lucy,	1735, s. d. Dec. 14, 1813.
Samuel,	1737.
John,	1744, m. Elizabeth Stone.

33

Dea. Daniel Leete, son of Dea. Pelatiah (15). m. June 14, 1738, Rhoda Stone, dau. of Caleb Stone and Sarah Meigs, of Guilford, born Nov. 2, 1719. He resided at Leete's Island, was a deacon in the 4th Congregational Church of Guilford, and died, aged 63, Oct. 1, 1772. His wife died, aged 50, Dec. 23, 1769.

84. Rhoda,	b.	April 14, 1739, m. Noah Rogers.
85. Daniel,		April 17, 1742, m. Charity Norton.
86. Ambrose,		Jan. 19, 1748, m. Miranda Chittenden.
87. Abraham,		Sept. 25, 1753, d. Oct. 26, 1753.
88. Abraham,		April 5, 1755, d. Nov. 5, 1757.

35

Dea. Pelatiah Leete, son of Dea. Pelatiah (15). m. Mar. 26, 1740, Lydia Cruttenden, dau. of Dea. Samuel Cruttenden and Mindwell Meigs, of Guilford, born Mar. 14, 1719. He was a deacon in the 4th Congregational Church of Guilford, and resided at Leete's Island. His wife died, aged 53, Aug. 13, 1772. He died, aged 73, May 28, 1786.

89. Pelatiah, b. Mar. 4, 1741, d. April 20, 1741.
90. Pelatiah, Aug. 22, 1744, m. Bethiah Norton.
91. (Lydia, Oct. 24, 1749, m. John Leete (108).
92. (Noah, Oct. 24, 1749, d. Oct. 21, 1769.
93. Eber, Mar. 25, 1752, d. Oct. 22, 1769.
94. Simeon, April 14, 1753, m. Zerviah Norton.
95. Amos, April 25, 1758, m. Hannah Ward.
96. Nathan, 1762, d. Nov. 1, 1769.

[NOTE.—Among the 44 persons who died of malignant epidemic dysentery in Guilford, in 1769, were 7 bearing the name of Leete: Abigail, wife of Pelatiah (15); Elizabeth, dau. of William (19); Rhoda, wife of Daniel (33); Noah, Eber, Nathan, sons of Pelatiah (35); Daniel, son of Daniel (85).—T.]

36 *Brewster*

Mehitabel Leete, dau. of Dea. Pelatiah (15), m. April 5, 1740, John Brewster. He died, aged about 65, May 27, 1789. She died, aged 56, Aug. 15, 1770.

Anna, b. Aug. 19, 1744.
John, Oct. 23, 1757.

40

Daniel Leete, son of Benjamin (17), m. Mehitabel Savelle, of New London. He was Captain of a vessel and resided in New London, dying there, aged 36, in 1757.

97. Sally, b. Jan. 6, 1755, s. d. Jan. 6, 1855, on her one hundredth birthday.

45

Levi Leete, son of Benjamin (17), m. Nov. 15, 1753, Lydia Hotchkin, widow of Joseph, and dau. of Theophilus Redfield and Priscilla Grinnell, of Killingworth, born Feb. 9, 1716. She died, aged 69, Dec. 16, 1784. He died, aged 38, Feb. 21, 1769. No children.

46

Sarah Leete, dau. of Benjamin (17), m. 1st, —— McKean, 2d, Stephen Leete (75).

42

Asa Leete, son of Benjamin (17), m. Oct. 19, 1748, Hannah Raynor, of Branford. They removed, about 1767, to Claremont, N. H., where he died. His descendants are still numerous in Claremont.

98.	Asa,	b. about	1749, m. Submit Bates.
99.	Ezekiel,	about	1751, m. Betsey Olney.
100.	Benjamin,	Jan. 17, 1753, m. Jane Meigs.	
101.	Sarah,	Dec. 24, 1754.	
102.	Adam Raynor,	Mar. 3, 1757, m. Tapher Thomas.	
103.	Levi,	1768, m. Abigail Olney.	
	Elizabeth.		
	Hannah.		

47   *Benton*

Leah Leete, dau. of Benjamin (17), m. May 28, 1758, Edward Benton, of Guilford, son of James Benton and Experience Stocker, born April 12, 1740. They removed to Albany, N. Y. He died, aged 54, Oct., 1794.

Jesse,	b. Dec. 1, 1759,	d. Aug. 8, 1760.
Clarinda,	May 23, 1761,	m. Wm. Hallock.
Chandler,	Jan. 31, 1764,	m. Mary Hall.
Rene,	Oct. 1, 1766,	m. —— Brewer.
Jesse,	Feb. 12, 1769.	
Ammi,	s.	

50   *Collins*

Margery Leete, dau. of Wm. (19), m. Oct. 20, 1731, Samuel Collins, of Guilford, son of John Collins and Ann Leete (11), born Nov. 2, 1704. He died in Guilford, aged 80, Dec. 6, 1784. She died, aged 91, Aug. 12, 1796.

    Margery, b. Mar. 14, 1732, m. Samuel Johnson.
    Anna,   Oct. 30, 1735, s. d. Nov. 12, 1803.
    Samuel,   June 6, 1737, s. d. Aug. 17, 1756.
    Gurdon,   Jan. 4, 1740, s.
    Thomas,   Jan. 18, 1742, s. d. Mar. 23, 1748.
    Charles,   July 31, 1744, s. d. Feb. 26, 1823.
    Sarai,   Jan. 11, 1748. m. James Amos.
    John Thomas, July 11, 1751, m. Submit Field.

48   *Hopson*

Ann Leete, dau. of Wm. (19), m. as 2d wife, Jan. 25, 1726, Samuel Hopson, of Guilford, born Jan. 10, 1684. They removed to Woodbury in 1750, and to Wallingford in 1760. He died, aged 88, Dec. 27, 1771.

    Ann,   b. Dec. 23, 1726.
    William,   May 3, 1729.
    Sarah,   June 29, 1731.
    Mary,   Aug. 4, 1737.
    Hannah,   April 2, 1740.
    John,   Sept. 29, 1741.
    Jordan,   Sept. 21, 1745.

51

Roland Leete, son of Wm. (19), m. Dec. 29, 1738, Mercy Dudley, dau. of Miles Dudley and Rachel Strong, of Guilford, born April 3, 1719. He died in Guilford, aged 59, Nov. 23, 1767.

104. Timothy, b.	Sept.	29, 1739, m. Mercy Cruttenden.
105. Ruth,	Nov.	7, 1740, m. Samuel Hoadley.
106. Anah,	July	6, 1742, m. Felix Norton.
107. Sarah,	July	11, 1744. s. d. Sept. 11, 1751.
108. John,	Jan.	16, 1746, m. Lydia Leete (91).
109. Asahel,	Nov.	10, 1747, d. Sept. 22, 1751.
110. Hannah,	Nov.	2, 1749, m. Josiah Howd.
111. Sarah,	Nov.	2, 1751, s. of Burlington, Vt.
112. Abner,		1753, died in camp, 1776.
113. Asahel,		1755, m. Polly Nott.
114. Miles,		1757, m. Betsey Hubbard.
115. Rachel,		m. Jonathan Hoadley.

52

William Leete, son of Wm. (19), was a graduate of Yale College in the class of 1733, and the only graduate bearing the Leete name previous to 1839. He died in Guilford, Sept. 21, 1756, aged 45. He was one of the victims of a terrible epidemic dysentery, which carried off thirty persons in Guilford in the two months of August and September, 1756. He was unmarried.

53

Jordan Leete, son of Wm. (19), m. Nov. 13, 1746, Rebecca Watrous. He resided in Guilford, and died, aged 52, April 8, 1773. His widow died Oct. 11, 1788.

116. Absalom, b.	Sept.	3, 1747, m. Jane Dudley.
117. Elizabeth,	Oct.	3, 1750, m. John Smith.
118. Amasa,	April	1, 1753, s. lost at sea about 1777.
119. Abraham,	April	5, 1755, s.
120. William,		1760, s. d. a Lieut. of an English frigate during Rev. war.

54

Solomon Leete, son of Wm. (19), m. Zipporah Stone, dau. of Samuel Stone and Mercy Rowlee, of Guilford, born April 28, 1720. She died, aged 80, June 25, 1800. He died, aged 81, Sept. 6, 1803.

 121. Solomon, b. Dec. 3, 1746, m. Hannah Norton.
 122. Thomas, Mar. 3, 1749, m. Anna Norton.
 123. James, Nov. 5, 1751, m. Jemima Cadwell.
 124. Elijah, Dec. 21, 1753, m. Betsey Brown.
 125. Ann, Jan. 4, 1756, s. d. Sept. 8, 1778.
 126. Pharez, Feb. 17, 1758, m. Ruth Savage.
 127. Abigail, Feb. 14, 1762, m. Calvin Chittenden.

60   *Hurd*

Dorothy Leete, dau. of Caleb (20), m. as 2d wife, Dec. 17, 1750, Daniel Hurd, of Killingworth. He died Jan. 1, 1763.

 Caleb Leete, b. 1753, m. Mary Griswold.
 Dorothy,   s. died aged 20.

61   *Hubbard*

Mercy Leete, dau. of Caleb (20), m. May 29, 1744, Jonathan Hubbard, of Glastonbury.

62   *Stone*

Rachel Leete, dau. of Caleb (20), m. May 16, 1749, Seth Stone, of Guilford, son of Ebenezer Stone and Hannah Norton, of Guilford, born in 1715. He died, aged 69, Aug. 3, 1784. She died, aged 83, Sept. 25, 1801.

 Andrew Leete, bap. Sept. 10, 1749, m. Mary Munger.
 Noah, bap. April 20, 1751, m. Martha Ludington.
 Rachel, " Jan. 21, 1753, m. David Crampton.
 Seth, " June 20, 1754, m. Anna Evarts.
 Rev. Wm., b. July 10, 1759, m. Tamsen Graves.
 Stephen, bap. April 15, 1762, s. d. June 24, 1782.

63   *Stone*

Sybil Leete, dau. of Samuel (21), m. Mar. 8, 1752, Ebenezer Stone, of Guilford, son of Ebenezer Stone and Hannah Norton, of Guilford, born Mar. 10, 1706. He died, aged 65, May 5, 1771. She died, aged 79, Aug. 31, 1803.

    Jerusha, bap. Feb. 18, 1753, m. Nathan Griswold.
    Levi,   1754, m. Mindwell Rice.
    Ebenezer,   1756, m. Jerusha ——.

64

Samuel Leete, son of Samuel (21), m. Dec. 20, 1752, Jane McNemor, who died, aged 30, Jan. 26, 1761, leaving one child. He m. 2d, July 23, 1761, widow Mary Kelly, who died, aged 39, Oct. 16, 1771, leaving 3 children. He m. 3d, Elizabeth Barber, dau. of Thomas Barber. He removed from Guilford to Canton, Conn., where he died, Dec. 7, 1799. His widow Elizabeth died, aged 85, in 1825.

    128. Jane,   b.   m Silas Case.
    129. Lucy,   Jan. 7, 1763. d. 1793, idiotic.
    130. Samuel,   1766, m. Sarah Case.
    131. Amos,   1769, m. Casamelia Mills.

66

Andrew Leete, son of Samuel (21), m. 1st, May 12, 1763, Esther Blatchley, dau. of Joseph Blatchley and Esther Collins, of Guilford, born Oct. 31, 1742. After her death he m. 2d, Submit Crockett, of Nova Scotia, Oct. 17, 1773. He was a Tory and removed to Nova Scotia.

    132. Jared,   m. Elizabeth Scranton.
    133. Andrew.
    134. Luranda, b.   1776, d. Dec. 23, 1822.
    135. Jabez.
    136. Submit.
    137. Lucretia.

67

Jared Leete, son of Samuel (21), m. Oct. 13, 1774, Hannah Hand, dau. of Joseph Hand and Hannah Hurlburt, of Guilford, born Dec. 28, 1753. Residence, Salisbury, Ct. and Williamstown, Mass.

138. Sarah, b. Feb. 25, 1776.
139. Mary, Aug. 1778, m. William Sweet.
140. Thomas Jordan, Oct. 31, 1781.
141. William, 1783, m. Mary Sweet.

68 *Barker*

Lucy Leete, dau. of Samuel (21), m. Nov. 27, 1760, Samuel Barker, of Branford.

73 *Ranney*

Chloe Leete, dau. of John (26), m. Jan. 31, 1754, Jeremiah Ranney.

David, b. Dec. 1, 1754.
Rebecca, May 22, 1757.
Rhoda, Aug. 28, 1758.

75

Stephen Leete, son of John (26), m. 2d, June 19, 1752, widow Sarah L. McKean, dau. of Benjamin Leete (17). She is No. 46. Residence, North Guilford.

[The first wife of Stephen Leete died without children May 6, 1749.]

142. Sarah, b. Sept. 27, 1755.
143. Mabel, April 8, 1757.
144. Calvin, 1759, killed by a fall, Jan. 13, 1774.

76

Submit Leete, dau. of John (26), m. Gershom Goodrich, of Middletown.

    Elias,   b. Nov. 12, 1758.
    Reuben,   Oct. 7, 1762.
    Elizabeth, Sept. 3, 1764.
    Lole,   Sept. 14, 1766.

77

Allen Leete, son of Gideon (28), m. 1st (name unknown), and had one son and three dau. He m. 2d, Oct. 21, 1779, Abigail Kelsey. He was drowned in Connecticut River, in 1783, while attempting to cross the river on the ice at Goodspeed's Landing. Residence, Chester, Ct.

  145. Abigail,   m. Abraham Waterhouse.
  146. Edward A., b. Oct. 6, 1761, m. Amy Morgan.
  147. Rachel,   m. —— Wynne.
  148. Cynthia,   m. —— Wynne.

78

Gideon Leete, son of Gideon (28), m. May 7, 1754, Ann Parmelee, dau. of John Parmelee and Sarah Boardman, of Durham, born Jan. 6, 1733. He resided for several years at Chester, Ct., but removed to Ohio about 1812.

  149. Sarah,   b. Nov. 1, 1755.
  150. Anna,   Oct. 13, 1757.
  151. Rebecca, Mar. 4, 1761.
  152. Lucy,   Nov. 3, 1763.
  153. Gideon,   Dec. 16, 1765. Removed to Ashtabula, O.
  154. Mary,   Aug. 11, 1767.

79

John Leete, son of Reuben (30), m. Dec. 12, 1787, Alpha Mann, dan. of Philip Mann and Ann Benton, of Guilford, born July 31, 1765. They went to West Bloomfield, N. Y., about 1800.

155. John,   b. Nov. 5, 1788, s. d. Aug. 2, 1838.
156. John Alfred,   Aug. 19, 1790, m. Sarah Story.
157. John Whiting, Feb. 6, 1795, s. d. Jan. 28, 1814.
158. John Sheldon, July 28, 1797, m. Caroline Stimson.
159. John Elliot,   April 1, 1800, m. Mehitabel Olmstead.
160. Alpha C.,   Sept. 22, 1802, m. Salmon Orcutt.
161. Lucy A.,   Feb. 9, 1806, m. David Conklin.
162. Amanda M.,   Aug. 18, 1808, m. Loring P. Day.

81   *Bishop*

Lucy Leete, dan. of Reuben (30), m. Jan. 1, 1777, Johnson Bishop, of Guilford, son of Enos Bishop and Abigail Burgis, of Guilford, born July 29, 1749. He died, aged 70, Jan. 25, 1820. She died, aged 60, May 4, 1813. Residence, Guilford. They had 4 children.

John,   b. May 9, 1778, d. Dec. 30, 1778.
Achsah, Dec. 17, 1780, m. Miner Bradley.
Lucy,   Mar. 9, 1784, m. Abel Kimberly.
Betsey, Oct. 22, 1789, s. d. Sept. 6, 1864.

82   *Handy*

Ruth Leete, dan. of Reuben (30), m. Jan. 26, 1774, Daniel P. Handy, of Guilford, son of Richard Handy and Anna Parmelee, born Feb. 6, 1748. He died Dec. 8, 1787.

Polly,   b. Aug. 7, 1775, m. Helmes Dewey.
Wealthy, Nov. 4, 1778.
Daniel, June 13, 1781, m. Lovisa Steele.
Joel,   Feb. 20, 1785.
Harriet, Dec. 25, 1786.

83

Sarah Leete, dau. of Reuben (30), m. —— Whitney.

84   Rogers

Rhoda Leete, dau. of Dea. Daniel (33), m. Oct. 23, 1765, Noah Rogers, of Cornwall, who went from Branford in 1760, son of Noah Rogers and Elizabeth Wheeler, of Branford, born May 8, 1732. He died, aged 78, in 1810.

Noah,	b. Oct. 13, 1766,	m. Lydia Cornwall.
Sarah,	June 24, 1768,	m. Oliver Burnham.
Rhoda,	Sept. 1770,	m. Andrew Cotter.
Abigail,	May 10, 1773,	m. Asahel Bradley.
Clarissa Irene,	May 2, 1779,	m. Prentice Williams.
Amanda,	Dec. 17, 1783,	m. Theodore Ives.

85

Daniel Leete, son of Dea. Daniel (33), m. Dec. 10, 1766, Charity Norton, dau. of Daniel Norton and Sarah Bradley, of Guilford, born in 1743. She died, aged 81, Feb. 13, 1824. He died, aged 83, May 3, 1825. Residence, Leete's Island.

163. Daniel,	b. Oct. 30, 1767,	d. Oct. 23, 1769.
164. Daniel,	Feb. 17, 1773,	m. Lydia Goldsmith.
165. Edmund,	May 10, 1775,	m. Fanny Goldsmith.
166. Rachel,	June 1, 1780,	m. John Goldsmith.

86

Dea. Ambrose Leete, son of Dea. Daniel (33), m. Nov. 10, 1773, Miranda Chittenden, dau. of Wm. Chittenden, of Guilford, and Rachel White, of Middletown, born Feb. 28, 1747. He was chosen a deacon of the Fourth Church in Guilford in 1786, and of the First Church in 1807. He died Feb. 14, 1809, aged 61. She died, aged 91, Sept. 16, 1838. They resided at Leete's Island.

167. Ambrose, b. Nov. 10, 1774, m. Catharine Ward.
168. Miranda, Jan. 8, 1777, s. d. Dec. 21, 1822.
169. Miner, June 30, 1779, m. Lucinda Norton.
170. Abraham, Jan. 1, 1784, s. d. Feb. 26, 1848.
171. Wealthy, Oct. 27, 1785, s. d. Mar. 23, 1870.

90

Pelatiah Leete, son of Dea. Pelatiah (35), m. June 17, 1767, Bethiah Norton, dau. of Thomas and Bethiah Norton, of Guilford. She died, aged 56, June 30, 1793. He m. 2d, Nov. 10, 1794, Mary Frisbie, of North Branford, who died, aged 76, Jan. 14, 1832. He died, aged 61, Mar. 2, 1806. Residence, Leete's Island.

172. Joel, b. April 15 1768, m. Molly Cruttenden.
173. Noah, Feb. 22, 1770, m. Huldah Ward.
174. Pelatiah, July 3, 1773, m. Betsey Ranney.
175. Mary, Feb. 15, 1798, m. Jude Ludington.

91

Lydia Leete, dau. of Dea. Pelatiah (35), m. Dec. 19, 1770, John Leete (108).

94

Simeon Leete, son of Dea. Pelatiah (35), m. Zerviah Norton, dau. of Thomas and Bethiah Norton, of Guilford. He was shot by the British in a skirmish at Leete's Island. The following is the inscription upon his tombstone: " In Memory of Mr. Simeon Leete who was shot by the Enemy at Leete's Island the 15th, and died the 19th, day of June 1781, in the 29th year of his age." His family removed, in 1802, to Fairfield, Herkimer County, N. Y., and afterward, in 1817, to Chautauqua County, N. Y., and to Erie County, Pa.

176. Anson, b. May 21, 1777, m. Abigail Dudley.
177. Augustus, Jan. 25, 1779, m. Naomi Winsow.
178. Simeon, 1781, m. Hannah Neely.

95

Amos Leete. son of Dea. Pelatiah (35), m. June 26, 1781, Hannah Ward, dau. of Thelus Ward and Lydia Franklin, of Guilford, born July 14, 1761. She died, aged 58, Dec. 10, 1819. He died, aged 50, April 15, 1808. Residence, Leete's Island.

179. Amanda, b. June 21, 1783, m. Ichabod Hand.
180. Eli, May 7, 1785, m. Zerviah Fowler.
181. Arta, Aug. 27, 1787, m. David Parmelee.
182. Amos, Jan. 8, 1790, m. Anna Leete (283).
183. Ward, Jan. 25, 1793, m. Sarah L. Campbell.
184. Harvey, Jan. 4, 1797, m. Sally Fowler.
185. Maria, Aug. 30, 1799, m. Leverett Cruttenden.
186. Sophia, Jan. 5, 1804, d. Mar. 4, 1806.

98

25. Feb. 1786

Asa Leete, son of Asa (42), m. Submit Bates. They resided in Claremont, N. H. It is thought they lived to bury all their children except Hannah, who married a Mr. Bishop, of Vermont. Their order of birth not known.

187. David.
188. Bates.
189. Miranda.
189½. Mitta.
190. Ira.
190½. Esther.
191. John.
192. Hannah, m. —— Bishop.
192½. Horace.

99

Ezekiel Leete, son of Asa (42), m. Betsey Olney. The order of birth in this family is not ascertained.

193. Andrew, m. Lucy Thomas.
194. Sarah.
195. Jerry.
196. Levi.
197. Elizabeth.
197½. Esther.
    Abigail.

100

Benjamin Leete, son of Asa (42), m. Jane Meigs, dau. of Ezekiel Meigs and Asenath Seward, born Dec. 5, 1756. They resided in Claremont, N. H. The sons are placed first in this family, without regard to the order of birth.

198. Daniel, m. Phebe Bailey.
199. Benjamin, m. Eunice Russell.
200. Lemuel, m. Abigail Tyler.
201. James, m. Philinda Rice.
202. John, b. Sept. 22, 1792. m. Fanny Thomas.
203. David, m. Matilda Rich.
204. Rachel, Mar. 11, 1781. m. Stephen Olney.
205. Susie, m. Benj. Grandy.
206. Sarah, m. Ebenezer Seaver.
207. Rhoda, s. d. aged 19.
208. Sylvia, m. Stephen Thomas.
209. Lucinda, m. John Thomas.
209½. Joel, m. { 1st. Mary Potter,
              { 2d. Rhoda Richardson.

102

Adam Raynor Leete, son of Asa (42), m. Tapher Thomas, b. 1759. He removed from Guilford with his father, to Claremont, N. H., about 1767, and subsequently to Shipton, Canada, in 1804, where he died, Sept. 13, 1824, aged 67. She died, aged 80, Feb. 26, 1840.

210. Ezra, b. Mar. 18, 1783, m. Sally Richardson.
211. Reuben, April 22, 1785, m. Polly Williamson.
212. Elizabeth, July 14, 1787, m. John Snell.
213. Chloe, May 5, 1791, m. Samuel Vesey.
214. Adam Raynor, May 16, 1794, m. Rachel Pope.
215. David Meigs, May 6, 1800, m. Polly Harvey.
216. Cyrus, July 27, 1802, m. Rebecca Pope.

103

Levi Leete, son of Asa (42), m. Abigail Olney. He removed to Canada in 1805, where he died Oct. 13, 1843, aged 74. She died 1854.

217. Alvah, b. May, 1801, m. Sarah M. Moore.
218. Hiram, m. Sophronia Burbank.
219. Timothy, d. aged 9 years.
220. Marenda, m. Moses Emerson.
221. Lucia, m. John Cassidy.
222. Almeda, m. Amos Brooks.

104

Timothy Leete, son of Roland (51), m. Mercy Cruttenden, dau. of Joseph Cruttenden and Lucy Spencer, of Guilford, born Oct. 16, 1737. They removed to Granville, Mass. He died in 1792, aged 53.

223. Nathan, b. Nov. 22, 1769.
224. Nathaniel, June 14, 1776, m. Dimis Wickham.
225. Ruth.
226. Ana, s. d. Sept. 20, 1846.
227. Abraham, m. Nabby Scofield.
228. Gaius.

105 *Hoadley*

Ruth Leete, dau. of Roland (51), m. Samuel Hoadley, of Branford.

Anah Leete, dau. of Roland (51), m. Felix Norton, son of Daniel Norton and Sarah Bradley, of Guilford.

  Joel, bap. April 12, 1764.
  Giles,   May 25, 1766.
  Ana,   July 3, 1768, d. Aug. 14, 1773.
  Linus,   1769.
  Medad,   1775.

108

John Leete, son of Roland (51), m. Dec. 19, 1770, Lydia Leete (91), dau. of Dea. Pelatiah Leete (35). They removed to Amenia and Stanford, N. Y. He died, aged 77, Dec., 1822. She died, aged 84, in 1833.

 229. John, b. Nov. 25, 1771, m. Artemisia Tompkins.
 230. Lydia,   Nov. 19, 1773, m. James Dudley.
 231. Amy,   Dec. 10, 1775, s. d. May 7, 1789.
 232. Lois,   April 11, 1778, m. Salmon Bunnell.
 233. Eber,   Oct. 8, 1780, m. Clarinda Gale.
 234. Olive,   Feb. 20, 1783, s. d. Oct. 14, 1833.
 235. Mina,   July 10, 1785, m. Joseph Carman.
 236. Orrit,   May 2, 1788, d. May 27, 1790.
 237. Orrit,   Oct. 12, 1790, s. d. May 23, 1828.
 238. Harvey, May 9, 1793, m. Almira Sayre.
 239. Eli,   Oct. 20, 1795, d. June 26, 1801.

110

Hannah Leete, dau. of Roland (51), m. Josiah Howd, June 18, 1767.

113

Asahel Leete, son of Roland (51), m. Polly Nott, born April 28, 1760. He removed to Granville, Mass., and Tinmouth, Vt. He died, aged 36, April, 1791. His widow died Aug., 1820.

240. Abner, b. 1799, s. killed by accident.
241. Sally, s.
242. John, 1783, m.
243. Noah, 1784, m. Welthy Mulford.
244. Thomas H., 1787, m. Phebe Collins.
245. Epaphras Nott, Jan. 28, 1798, m. Harriet W. Thompson.
246. Semantha, 1790, d. y.

114

Miles Leete, son of Roland (51), m. Betsey Hubbard. He removed to Vermont, and to Peru, Clinton County, N. Y. He died, aged 77, July 4, 1834.

247. Lois, b. Oct. 16, 1792, m. Elmore Gould.
248. Russell, Nov. 10, 1795, m. Polly Kingsley.
249. Roxana, d. aged 6.
250. Harvey H., Feb. 21, 1798, m. Harriet Hotchkin.
251. Nancy.
252. Almon, Feb. 22, 1800, m. Sarah Beardsley.
253. John G., May 10, 1802, m. Amy Ketcham.
254. Henry, Mar. 18, 1805, m. Ruth N. Grover.
255. Roxana, Aug. 19, 1806, m. James P. Goodwin.
256. Wealthy, Nov. 1, 1868, m. Apollos Goodwin.
257. Elizabeth, Nov. 17, 1811, m. Richard Fitz Gerald.

115 *Hoadley*

Rachel Leete, dau. of Roland (51), m. Jonathan Hoadley, of Branford.

116

Absalom Leete, son of Jordan (53), m. Jane Dudley, dau. of Samuel Dudley and Jane Talman, of Guilford, born Feb. 14, 1745. They resided in East Guilford, and died within six days of each other. She died, aged 55, Oct. 21, 1800. He died, aged 53, Oct. 27, 1800.

258. Amasa,   b.   1770, m. Abigail Stone.
259. Linus,   Mar. 17, 1777, m. Betsey Dudley.
260. Lovicia,   1781, s. d. Jan. 10, 1831.
261. Absalom,   June 17, 1782, m. Sally Pease.

117   *Smith*

Elizabeth Leete, dau. of Jordan (53), m. John Smith, Jan., 1772.

121

Solomon Leete, son of Solomon (54), m. Nov. 3, 1772, Hannah Norton, dau. of Daniel Norton and Sarah Bradley, of Guilford. They removed to Granville, N. Y., and to Tioga County, Pa. He died, aged 76, in 1822. She died, aged 70, Sept. 22, 1820.

262. Henry,   m. Andrea Jackson.
263. Parnella.   m. Oliver Greatrash.
264. Dr. Frederic,   m. Lucy Morse.
265. Orpha,   d. aged 24.
266. William,   m. Susan Humphrey.
267. Uriah,   m. Mary Ives.
268. Abner,   m. Polly Remsen.
269. Thomas,   m. Hannah Ives.
270. Betsey,   s.
271. Anna,   s.

122

Thomas Leete, son of Solomon (54), m. June 30, 1773, Anna Norton, dau. of Daniel Norton and Sarah Bradley, of Guilford, born in 1751. They resided in Guilford and had no children. He died, aged 81, May 27, 1830. She died, aged 83, Feb. 15, 1834. He was an eccentric and somewhat original character. He called people by their Christian names. Rev. Aaron Dutton, his minister, he addressed as Aaron, and spoke of him in the same way. He avoided titles and surnames. Although a member of the First Church of Guilford, in the last years of his life, instead of attending church he had services of his own, and during the hours of public worship on Sunday would go through the forms of singing, prayer and preaching in his own house with only his wife for his audience. The next day he would speak of his interview with Luke, John or Paul.

123

James Leete, son of Solomon (54), m. Jan. 27, 1774, Jemima Cadwell. He resided in Guilford, and was drowned April 3, 1793, aged 41. She died Nov. 26, 1802, aged 48.

272. Dolly, b. 1774, d. Feb. 13, 1779.
273. Anna, 1776, d. Jan. 27, 1788.
274. James, 1777, m. Zibeah Miller.
275. Juliana, Mar. 28, 1775, m. Benjamin Bradley.
276. Peter, 1790, m. Freelove Maynard.

124

Elijah Leete, son of Solomon (54), m. Betsey Brown, of Southold, L. I., who died, aged 30, Aug. 28, 1782, leaving one child. He m. 2d, Leah Truby, widow of Giles Truby and dau. of Geo. Hill and Ruth Robinson, of Guilford, born June 19, 1748, who died, aged 70, Feb. 11, 1818, leaving three children. He m. 3d, Ruth Leete, widow of Pharez Leete (126), née Savage, who died, aged 66, July 6, 1822. He died in Guilford, aged 71, April 19, 1825.

277. Daniel Brown, b. Aug. 21, 1781, m. Electa Fowler.
278. Samuel,   April 15, 1787, m. Julia Frisbie.
279. Clarissa,   Aug. 6, 1789, m. Bela Stone.
280. Betsey,   June 20, 1793, m. James H. Moore.

126

Pharez Leete, son of Solomon (54), m. Nov. 12, 1780, Ruth Savage. He removed to North Haven and died in 1820 aged 62. His widow m. for 2d husband Elijah Leete (124). She died, aged 66, July 6, 1822.

281. George, b. Mar. 29, 1782, m. Experience Elliot.
282. Ruth,   Dec. 19, 1785, m. Nymphias Stacey.
283. ⎰ Anna,   May 5, 1791, m. Amos Leete (182).
284. ⎱ Harvey,   May 5, 1791, d. Sept. 2, 1791.

127   *Chittenden*

Abigail Leete, dan. of Solomon (54), m. Mar. 18, 1793, Calvin Chittenden, of Guilford, son of William Chittenden and Sarah Stevens, born Mar. 18, 1755. They removed to Richmond, Mass., where he died, aged 80, May 1, 1835. She died, aged 73, Dec. 19, 1834.

Wm. Stevens, b. Dec. 31, 1793.
James L.,   1795, m. Clarissa Kilbourn.
Anna,   m. Sylvester Tracy.

128   *Case*

Jane Leete, dan. of Samuel (64), m. Silas Case, of Canton.

Kelly, b.   1777.

130

Samuel Leete, son of Samuel (64), m. Sarah Case, dan. of Jesse Case and Sarah Humphrey, of West Simsbury, born Dec. 4, 1768.

131

Amos Leete, son of Samuel (64), m. Casamelia Mills, dau. of Benjamin Mills and Hannah Humphrey, born April 17, 1770. He was born in Guilford, removed to Canton, Connecticut, with his father, and about 1820 removed to Vienna, Trumbull Co., Ohio, where he died aged 83.

285.	Flora,	m. Alexander Tanner.
286.	Homer,	m. Emily Woodford.
287.	Trumbull,	m. Harriet Lewis.
288.	Emily,	m. Rastus Griffing.
289.	Julia,	m. Horatio Meacham.
290.	Sherman,	m. Sarah Truesdal.
290½.	George,	m. Jane Chew.

132

Jared Leete, son of Andrew (66), m. Nov. 29, 1784, Elizabeth Scranton, dau. of Timothy Scranton, of Guilford, and Abigail Torrey, of Boston, born Nov. 6, 1757. She died, aged 66, Jan. 4, 1824. He m., 2d, widow Lois Hart, Oct. 2, 1833. She died April 6, 1851. He died Oct. 23, 1844.

291. Elizabeth, b. Sept. 2, 1785, m. Amasa Stevens.
292. Jared, April, 1787, m. Lydia Cook.
293. Ruth, 1790, m. Titus Cook.
294. Simeon, 1792, m. Eliza Hotchkiss.
295. Lucy, 1794, m. Oziel Wilcox.
296. James A., June 23, 1796, m. Hannah Cone.
297. Alexander, Oct., 1797, m. Sally Coe.

139

Mary Leete, dau. of Jared (67), m. William Sweet, of Williamstown, Mass.

141

William Leete, son of Jared (67), m. Mary Sweet.

298. Mary,	b. Jan.,	1806.	
299. Samuel H.,	Jan.,	1810.	
300. Hannah,	April,	1813.	
301. Alonzo,	Jan.	5, 1817, m. Laura Hill.	
302. Luther,	July,	1819, m. Chloe Hill.	[a raft.
303. Joseph,	Oct.,	1821, d. about 1833; killed upon	

146

Edward A. Leete, son of Allen (77), m. in 1793, Amy Morgan, dau. of John Morgan and Eunice Casey, of Preston, Connecticut. He resided in Chester, Connecticut, where he died, aged 80, Mar., 1841.

304. Samuel M.,	b. Sept. 3, 1794, m. Anna Atwood.
305. John C.,	Nov. 25, 1797, m. Lydia Shipman.
306. Elizabeth,	Feb. 22, 1799, d. y.
307. Emily A.,	Aug. 11, 1801, s. d. 1841.
308. Eliza A.,	June 11, 1803, m. Joseph Haswell.
309. Edw. A., Jr.,	Aug. 11, 1805, m. Mary W. Keller.
310. Eunice C.,	Sept. 27, 1807, m. Charles Young.

156

John Alfred Leete, son of John (79), m. Jan. 10, 1816, Sarah Story, of Goshen, N. H., born July 2, 1793. She died, aged 82, Feb. 13, 1876. He died, aged 71, April 29, 1862. Residence, West Bloomfield, N. Y.

311. Geo. A.,	b. Jan. 31, 1817, m. Mary J. Hall.
312. Cynthia E.,	Mar. 1, 1819, m. Hiram Wilcox.
313. Ira O.,	April 8, 1821, m. Helena Ham.
314. Charles L.,	April 30, 1823, m. Mary Benton.

158

John Sheldon Leete, son of John (79), m. Caroline Stimson.

315. Mary.
316. Lucius.

159

John Elliot Leete, son of John (79), m. Mehitabel Olmstead.

317. Alpha.
318. Harley E.
319. Clarissa.
320. Lucy.
321. Mary A.
322. Lorenzo.
323. Salmon.

160   *Orcutt*

Alpha C. Leete, dau. of John (79), m. Mar. 2, 1831, Salmon Orcutt, of Victor, N. Y. She died, aged 77, March 12, 1880.

Ann M.,	m. George Stafford.
Ermina,	d. y.
John A.,	d. y.
Cynthia,	d. y.

161   *Conklin*

Lucy A. Leete, dau. of John (79), m. David Conklin. They removed to Wisconsin. She died, aged 74, in 1880.

Seraph,	m. Charles Dudley.
Fausta.	
David.	
Maron,	m. P. G. Gardner.

162

Amanda M. Leete, dau. of John (79), m. in 1828 Loring P. Day, of Lockport, N. Y.

    Charles, b. July 21, 1831, m. Sarah L. Wilcox.
    Myron, May 31, 1834.
    Geo. Mann, July 22, 1846, m. Hattie O. Milton.

164

Daniel Leete, son of Daniel (85), m. April 17, 1794, Lydia Goldsmith, dau. of John Goldsmith and Deborah Terry, born in Durham, Conn., July 1, 1774. She died, aged 68, Oct. 19, 1842. He died, aged 79, Aug. 17, 1846. They resided at Leete's Island, and had no children.

165

Edmund Leete, son of Daniel (85), m. Feb. 26, 1801, Fanny Goldsmith, dau. of John Goldsmith and Mary Case, of Guilford, born Feb. 25, 1783. Residence, Leete's Island. He died, aged 50, May 28, 1825. She died, aged 82, Dec. 5, 1864.

  324. Henry Wm., b. Dec. 1, 1801, m. Nancy Doolittle.
  325. Benj. Case, Sept. 23, 1804, m. Amanda Cook.
  326. Fanny Minerva, Nov. 8, 1806, m. George Fowler.
  327. Samuel Willis, July 17, 1809, m. Emma Buell.
  328. Mary Fidelia, Nov. 24, 1811, m. Russell Crampton.
  329. Eunice Louisa, Dec. 8, 1817, m. Philander Field.

166

Rachel Leete, dau. of Daniel (85), m. Dec. 21, 1812, John Goldsmith, of Guilford, son of John Goldsmith and Mary Case, of Guilford, born Oct. 20, 1785. He died, aged 54, April 4, 1840. She died, aged 86, April 26, 1866. They resided in Guilford, and had no children.

167

Ambrose Leete, son of Dea. Ambrose (86), m. Feb. 21, 1802, Catharine Ward, dau. of Thelus Ward and Sarah Shelley, of Guilford, born Sept. 22, 1780. She died, aged 69, Jan. 5, 1850. He died, aged 74, May 19, 1849. They resided at Leete's Island.

330. Sidney Washington, b. Nov. 19, 1802, m. Susan Atwater.
331. Albert Augustus, b. Oct. 11, 1805, m. Betsey A. Parmelee.
332. Harriet, Feb. 14, 1808, m. John E. Fowler.
333. Ambrose Ward, Oct. 22, 1809, m. Abigail M. Leete
334. Catharine Ward, June 9, 1811. [(698).
335. Miranda Cornelia, Feb. 20, 1814, m. Hez'kiah Parmelee.
336. Charles Frederic, Dec. 7, 1820, m. Martha H. W. Lay.

169
~~168~~

Miner Leete, son of Dea. Ambrose (86), m. Nov. 17, 1807, Lucinda Norton, dau. of Col. Rufus Norton and Hannah Cook, of Guilford, born Nov. 18, 1780. They resided at Leete's Island where he died, aged 47, Nov. 7, 1826. She died, aged 67, Aug. 28, 1848.

337. Edward Lorenzo, b. June 28, 1810, m. Sylvia Fowler.
338. Rufus Norton, Aug. 17, 1812, m. Sarah Bishop.
339. Theodore Adgate, May 18, 1814, m. Mary C. White.
340. Calvin Miner, Oct. 18, 1816, m. L. M. Leete (705).
341. Louisa Maria, Aug. 20, 1822, s. d. July 29, 1855.

172

Joel Leete, son of Pelatiah (90), m. May 27, 1790, Molly Cruttenden, dau. of Noah Cruttenden and Naomi Atwell, of Guilford, born Aug. 25, 1765. Residence, Leete's Island. He died, aged 73, Jan. 28, 1842. She died, aged 78, Nov. 27, 1843.

342. Alvan,   b. Aug. 24, 1791. m. Rebecca Butler.
343. Polly Maria,   Mar. 7, 1794. d. Jan. 3, 1795.
344. Morris Atwell,   Nov. 10, 1795, m. Clarinda Graves.
345. Frederic Wm.,   July 6, 1803. m. S. J. Fowler.

173

Noah Leete, son of Pelatiah (90), m. Feb. 22, 1792, Huldah Ward, dau. of Thelus Ward and Lydia Franklin, of Guilford, born Feb. 14, 1774. They resided first at Leete's Island, afterward at Verona, N. Y. He died, aged 57, in 1827. She died, aged 63, in 1837.

346. Allen Norton, b. Mar. 6, 1793. m. Isabella Murden.
347. Lydia Meigs,   Mar. 3, 1796. m. Jas. Russiquia.
348. Chas. Ward,   Oct. 14, 1799. m. Adeline Loomis.
349. Harley Nelson,   m. Betsey B. Leete (351).
350. Artemisia,   m. Solomon Hess.

174

Pelatiah Leete, son of Pelatiah (90), m. May 28, 1797, Betsey Ranney, dau. of Reuben and Lucinda Ranney, of Guilford, born Mar. 20, 1771. They removed to Verona, N. Y.

351. Betsey Bethiah, b. April 12, 1798. m. H. N. Leete (349).
352. Sophia Maria,   May 18, 1802. m. Justyn Whaley.
353. Myrta Maritta, Oct. 4, 1804. m. Hiram Edes.
354. Amanda Jennette, Oct. 16, 1807. m. Otis Pratt.
355. Laura Ann,   May 31, 1810, s. d.
356. Sarah Ward,   Jan. 9, 1813. m. Elias Benedict.
357. Pelatiah Ward, May   4, 1815, m. Elizabeth Fuller.

175   *Ludington*

Mary Leete, dau. of Pelatiah (90), m. Oct. 6, 1823, Jude Ludington, of West Springfield, Mass., born May 23, 1788. He died, aged 66, Feb. 26, 1855. She m. 2d, Oct. 22, 1856, Henry Fuller. She died, aged 81, Aug. 2, 1879.

176

Capt. Anson Leete, son of Simeon (94), m. in 1799 Abigail Dudley, dau. of Jonathan Dudley and Elizabeth Hill, of Guilford, born Jan. 27, 1780. He went to Herkimer County, N. Y., in 1802, and to Chantauqua County, N. Y., in 1817. He died, aged 66, in 1843. She died, aged 99, Feb. 2, 1879.

358. Jonathan Dudley, b. Jan. 24, 1800, m. Lucy Hanchett.
359. Simeon, b. Sept. 18, 1801, m. Harriet Weed.
360. Timothy, April 16, 1803, m. Cynthia Kennedy.
361. Lewis, Nov. 29, 1805, m. Mary Thumb.
362. Eliza, Nov. 19, 1807, m. Nehemiah Herrick.
363. Caroline, Aug. 16, 1810, m. Wm. Vorce.
364. Maria, May 30, 1812, m. John Mason, Esq.
365. Franklin, July 20, 1815, m. Sally Sumner.
366. William, June 24, 1818, m. Eliza A. Strong.
367. Mary, Sept. 1, 1820, m. Henry Barnhart.

In the spring of 1817 Capt. Leete bought at the Land Office, for $4.50 per acre, the tract of land embracing the now famous Chantauqua Point. From this time until 1875 it was known as Leete's Point. It then passed into the possession of the Point Chautauqua Association, and took its present name.

177

Augustus Leete, son of Simeon (94), m. in 1806, Naomi Winsow. He went to Herkimer Co., N. Y., in 1802, and to Erie Co., Penn., in 1811. He died in 1863, aged 84.

368. Emeline W., b. May 8, 1807, m. Robert Caldwell.
369. Matheson W., Feb. 15, 1810, m. Betsey Coombs.
370. Minerva, Nov. 5, 1813.
371. Lydia Z., Feb. 2, 1818, m. Zenas Rogers.
372. Larned H., April 15, 1821, s. d. 1841.

178

Simeon Leete, son of Simeon (94), m. Hannah Neeley. Residence, Harbor Creek, Erie Co., Pa.

373. Amanda,	b.	1816, m. Joseph McCord.
374. Alfred N.,		1818, m. Harriet Hampson.
375. Calvin,		1819, m. Eleanor Elliot.
376. Susan,		1821.
377. Matilda,		1822, m. J. R. Moorhead.
378. Ann,		1824, m. Plara Elliot.
379. John,		1829, s. d. 1855.

179   *Hand*

Amanda Leete, dau. of Amos (95), m. Ichabod Hand, of Oneida, N. Y., as his 2d wife. He died, aged 63, Mar. 12, 1846.

Hannah Ward, b.	Jan. 28, 1812, m. Orville Knox.
George Edward,	Aug. 7, 1813, s. d at sea, 1841.
Theo. Francis,	Aug. 14, 1815, m. E. Higgenbottom.
Sidney Graves,	Dec. 24, 1821, of Baltimore.
Henry Hobert,	Sept. 28, 1824, d. Mar. 29, 1875.

180

Eli Leete, son of Amos (95), m. Zerviah Fowler, dau. of Josiah Fowler and Zerviah Kirkham, of Northford, baptized June 3, 1790. He died at Leete's Island, aged 46, Oct. 20, 1831. He died of suffocation in attempting to swallow a piece of meat.

380. Nancy Urania,	b.	1813, s. d. Dec. 16, 1830.
381. Elizabeth,	April,	1816, m. James Minor.
382. Caroline A.,		1820, m. Warren Walkley.
383. Sereno Fowler,		1822, born with one arm.
384. Maria.		

181

Arta Leete, dau. of Amos (95), m. May 24, 1807, David Parmelee, son of David Parmelee and Asenath Kirkham, of Guilford, born Oct. 3, 1784. She died, aged 29, Oct. 19, 1816. He m. a 2d and a 3d wife and died in Guilford, Aug. 6, 1870, aged 86.

    Benjamin, b. Aug. 17, 1808, drowned May 15, 1817.
    Samuel W., Aug. 22, 1810, m. Catharine Rouke.
    David Kirtland, Sept. 4, 1812, m. Sarah E. Stone.

182

Amos Leete, son of Amos (95), m. Anna Leete (283), dau. of Pharez (123). He died, aged 46, Feb. 22, 1836. She died, aged 62, July 14, 1853.

    385. Wm. Pharez, b. Sept. 23, 1821, m. E. Goodrich.
    386. Ruth, Aug. 5, 1823, m. Alvan B. Rose.
    387. Anna, Jan. 3, 1826, m. Samuel L. Hall.
    388. Hannah Ward, Nov. 22, 1827, m. R. Ward Benton.
    389. Amos Harvey, Aug. 6, 1833, m. Sarah A. Way.

183

Ward Leete, son of Amos (95), m. widow Sarah L. Campbell. He resided in New York, and died there, aged 84, in June, 1877. His widow, Sarah Louise, died August 21, 1882. Buried at Leete's Island. No children.

184

Harvey Leete, son of Amos (95), m. Jan. 28, 1818, Sally Fowler, dau. of Bela Fowler and Clarissa Hilliard, of Guilford, born Oct. 16, 1800. She died, aged 20, Oct. 21, 1820. After her death he removed to Fayetteville, N. C., where he m. June, 1823, Sarah Ann Cook, born Feb. 1, 1800.

He engaged in mercantile business, and was an exemplary and active member of the Presbyterian church in Fayetteville, and for many years a ruling elder in it. He died Jan. 23, 1852, aged 55 years. She died, aged 72, May 30, 1872.

390. Clarissa M.,   b. July 25, 1818, m. Dr. J. C. Hepburn.
391. Sarah,   Sept. 12, 1820, s. d. Sept. 12, 1840.
392. Charles Edward, April 6, 1824, d. Aug. 25, 1826.
393. Charles Edward, Nov. 24, 1826, m. Sarah L. Hawley.
394. William James, Feb. 21, 1828, m. in Texas.
395. Isabella Amanda, Feb. 10, 1830, Missionary to Japan.
396. John Henry,   Aug. 10, 1833, d. June 9, 1836.
397. John Henry,   Nov. 1, 1837, s. d. May 30, 1866.

185 *Cruttenden*

Maria Leete, dau. of Amos (95), m. Leverett Cruttenden, of Lansingburg, N. Y., son of Timothy Cruttenden and Parnell Redfield, of Guilford. They went to Verona, N. Y., and afterward to Ohio.

192 *Bishop*

Hannah Leete, dau. of Asa (98), m. a Mr. Bishop, of Jericho, Vermont, and had 2 sons and 3 daughters. Names of daughters unknown. Sons—

Leete.
Daniel.

193

Andrew Leete, son of Ezekiel (99), m. Lucy Thomas, eldest daughter of Zara Thomas.

398. Reuben T.
399. Cyrus A.
400. Henry.
401. Dau.
402. Dau.
403. Dau.

198

Daniel Leete, son of Benjamin (100), m. Phebe Bailey.

404. Daniel.
405. William.

Probably more. Daniel and William moved west many years ago.

199

Benjamin Leete, son of Benjamin (100), m. Eunice Russell.

406. Benjamin, b. Dec., 1809, m. Jane E. Richardson.
407. Charles.
408. Louisa.
409. Susan,   m. Charles Webber.
410. Russell.
410½. Sarah.
411. Lemuel.
412. Philinda,   m. Franklin Leonard.
413. Geo. W.
414. Eunice,   m. Adam Wilson.

200

Lemuel Leete, son of Benjamin (100), m. Abigail Tyler and died without children.

201

James Leete, son of Benjamin (100), m. about 1814, Philinda Rice.

415. Maria, m. Charles Ellis.
416. Jane, m. Lewis W. Randall
417. James, m. Lucy Ann Maynard.
418. John.
419. Charles, m. Frances Ann Holden.
420. Edwin, m. Fidelia Bliss.
421. Abby C., m. Carl Royce.

202

John Leete, son of Benjamin (100), m. Feb. 11, 1817, Fanny Thomas. He lived in Claremont, N. H., and died there.

422. Rhoda, b. May 26, 1819, m. Hamden Kidder.
423. Lucretia, Aug. 12, 1820, m. Elisha Marston.
423½. Laurinda, Sept. 12, 1822, d. young.
424. Frederic, Aug. 22, 1826, m. Susan Combs.
425. John, Oct. 25, 1828, m. Sarah Green.
426. Lemuel, Sept. 4, 1830, m. Mary Green.

203

David Leete, son of Benjamin (100), m. 1st, Matilda Rich, 2d, Martha Pierce. Two children.

427. Ellen.
428. Another.

204 *Olney*

Rachel Leete, dau. of Benjamin (100), m. Stephen Olney, of Canada, and had a large family. She had 14 children, 66 grandchildren, 46 great-grandchildren, and 4 great-great-grandchildren in her lifetime. She died, aged 97, Oct. 14, 1878.

205 *Grandy*

Susie Leete, dau. of Benjamin (100), m. Benj. Grandy and had a large family.

206 *Seaver*

Sarah Leete, dau. of Benjamin (100), m. Ebenezer Seaver. Left 3 children.

208 *Thomas*

Sylvia Leete, dau. of Benjamin (100), m. Stephen Thomas. He died, and she m. 2d, —— Judkins. 8 children; 5 by first marriage, 3 by last.

209 *Thomas*

Lucinda Leete, dau. of Benjamin (100), m. 1st, John Thomas. He died. She m. 2d, Mr. Sturtevant. 5 children; 4 by first marriage, 1 by second. She died, aged 84, April 22, 1883.

209½

Joel Leete, son of Benjamin (100), m. 1st, Mary Potter, and 2d, Rhoda Richardson. Family not ascertained.

210

Ezra Leete, son of Adam Raynor (102), m. Sally Richardson. He died in 1843, aged 60.

429. Dexter, b. Jan. 29, 1809, m. Jane Bayne.
430. Lemuel, d. aged 20.
431. Ezra, m.
432. Phebe, d. young.

211

Reuben Leete, son of Adam Raynor (102), m. in 1810 Polly Williamson. He resided in Shipton, P. Q., Canada, where his descendants still live. He fell dead while raking hay in the field, Aug. 11, 1859, aged 74.

433. Reuben, b. Aug. 12, 1814, m. Elvira L. Andrews.
434. Geo. Washington, b. Feb. 24, 1819, m. L. Williamson.
435. Clarissa, b. July 12, 1823, m. Wellington Willey.
436. William, Sept. 5, 1826, m. Caroline Willey.
437. Belinda, Aug. 15, 1828, m. James H. Barnum.

212 *Snell*

Elizabeth Leete, dau. of Adam Raynor, m. John Snell and had 4 children.

Phebe.
Mamry.
Adam R.
Christopher.

213 *Vesey*

Chloe Leete, dau. of Adam Raynor (102), m. Samuel Vesey and had 9 children.

Eliza.
John.
Nancy.
Benjamin.
William.
Jane.
Walter.
Gilman.
Nelson.

214

Adam Raynor Leete, son of Adam R. (102), m. Rachel Pope. He died Nov. 24, 1878, aged 82. Residence, Shipton, P. Q., Canada.

438. Tapher,   b. Jan. 16, 1819, m. Wooster Willey.
439. Rachel,   Feb. 18, 1823, m. John Olney.
440. Adam Raynor, June 26, 1832, m. Flora Magoon.
441. Chloe A.   Oct. 30, 1839, m. Moses W. Hall.

215

David M. Leete, son of Adam R. (102), m. Polly Harvey. He died, aged 75, Jan. 18, 1876. Residence, Shipton, Canada.

442. Norman,   b. July 19, 1829, d. March 22, 1848.
443. Adam Raynor, Dec. 27, 1830, m. Louisa C. Gage.
444. Eleanor,   Mar. 30, 1836, m. Avery Denison.

216

Cyrus Leete, son of Adam R. (102), m. Rebecca Pope. He died, aged 80, March 8, 1883.

445. Asa,   b. Oct. 2, 1825, m. Mary Morse.
446. Phebe,   Aug. 28, 1827, m. Avery Green.
447. Loren,   Nov. 9, 1830, m.
448. Cyrus,   Mar. 1, 1836, m. Dorothy B. Bohanon.
449. Henry,   Nov. 3, 1840, m. Sarah Leavitt.

217

Alvah Leete, son of Levi (103), m. Sarah M. Moore. He died, aged 78, in 1879. She died, aged 72, in 1877.

450. Timothy, b. Dec. 31, 1827, m. Mary Ann Mahaffy.
451. Sarah Mahala, 1830, m. William Adams.
452. James, 1834, m. Maria Doyle.
453. John, 1837, m. Margaret A. Greer.
454. Simeon, 1840, m. Marg't A. Andrews.
454¼. Mary Annis, 1843, d. aged 11.
454½. Hiram, 1847, m. Mary Dickey.

218

Hiram Leete, son of Levi (103), m. Sophronia Burbank.

455. Abigail, b. 1830, m. Josiah Kenerson.
456. Levi, 1833, m. Killed in battle.
457. Freeman, 1836, m. in Massachusetts.

220 *Emerson*

Marenda Leete, dau. of Levi (103), m. Moses Emerson.
    Alma.
    Hiram.
    Miriam.
    Jasper.
    Lucia.

221 *Cassidy*

Lucia Leete, dau. of Levi (103), m. John Cassidy.

222 *Brooks*

Almeda Leete, dau. of Levi (103), m. Amos Brooks.

224

Dea. Nathaniel Leete, son of Timothy (104), m. Feb. 2, 1800, Dimis Wickham, of Haddam, Conn., and spent all his married life at West Stockbridge, Mass. Here he owned a large farm, upon which was a valuable iron-ore bed called "Leete's ore bed." He was a deacon of the church in West Stockbridge, and used "the office of a deacon well." He was beloved while living, and his memory is blessed. He died, aged 72, Sept., 1848.

458. Betsey, b. Dec. 25, 1800, m. Joseph King.
459. Horace, Nov. 25, 1803, m. Elizabeth Caul.
460. Chauncey, Feb. 11, 1806, m. Mary Ward.
461. Sophia, Oct. 29, 1810, m. Ashman Benedict.
462. Clarinda, Dec. 11, 1814, m. Myron M. Beebe.
463. Sarah, Aug. 6, 1816, m. Charles Dudley.
464. Edna, Mar. 8, 1819, m. Calvin Salls.
465. Olive, April 29, 1823, m. John C. Clark.

227

Abraham Leete, son of Timothy (104), m. Nabby Scofield, of Litchfield, Conn., by whom he had a daughter.

466. Lucy, m. Daniel Loper.

229

John Leete, son of John (108), m. March, 1819, Artemisia Tompkins. He resided in Stanford, N. Y., and died without children, Oct. 27, 1830, aged 59.

230 *Dudley*

Lydia Leete, dau. of John (108), m. May 1st, 1805, James Dudley, of Richmond, Mass., son of John Dudley and Tryphena Stone, born Nov. 19, 1772. He removed, in 1833, to Ulster County, N. Y., where he died, aged 62, Jan. 26, 1835. She died, aged 68, Aug. 20, 1842.

Chester,   b. July 4, 1806, s. d. 1879.
Geo. Anson,   1808, d. 1809.
Geo. Anson,   June 14, 1810, m. Sarah Tuthill.
James Harvey, July 14, 1817, m. Charlotte Wiltsie.

232   *Bunnell*

Lois Leete, dau. of John (108), m. May 25, 1804, Salmon Bunnell. They went to Susquehanna Co., Pa., where she died, aged 72, Sept. 7, 1850.

    Myron L., b. April 4, 1805.
    Theron B.,   Nov. 12, 1808.
    Ruth L.,   Feb. 10, 1810.
{ John T.,   Jan. 11, 1813.
{ Alexander H.,   Jan. 11, 1813.
    Salmon B.,   Dec. 10, 1815, d. Aug. 3, 1837.

233

Eber Leete, son of John (108), m. Sept. 9, 1801, Clarinda Gale. He died, aged 68, Nov. 20, 1848. Residence, New York City.

467. Dr. Albert Ely, b. July 1, 1802, m. Catharine Palen.
468. Clarinda,   b. Mar. 16, 1804, m. B. K. Burton.
469. Almira.   July 10, 1809, s. d. July 9, 1864.
470. Edgar Josiah, Mar. 12, 1811. Lawyer, N. Y. City.

235   *Carman*

Mina Leete, dau. of John (108), m. Mar. 10, 1813, Joseph Carman, of Cairo, N. Y. She died, Sept. 12, 1833, aged 48.

    John,   b. Mar. 1, 1815.
    Lydia L.,   June 18, 1816.
    Joseph G.,   1819.

238

Harvey Leete, son of John (108), m. June 4, 1832, Almira Sayre. She died, leaving one child. He m. 2d, Oct. 27, 1850, widow —— Mattoon. He resided in Cairo, N. Y.

471. J. Sayre, b. April 21, 1833, m.

242

John Leete, son of Asahel (113), m. and died a young man.

243

Noah Leete, son of Asahel (113), m. Weltha Mulford, born Aug. 5, 1786. She died, aged 58, July 10, 1844. He died, aged 76, July 24, 1860.

472. Asahel, b. May 19, 1812, m. Emeline Grace Fowler.
473. Harriet Sabrina, b. Sept. 22, 1816, m. Alex. H. Fenner.
474. Lucretia, b. April 13, 1820, m. Bela Fenner.
475. Weltha, Sept. 13, 1822, m. Harlow Jackson.
476. Mary A., Aug. 4, 1824, Butler Morley.
477. Martha, Oct. 13, 1826, m. Jesse D. Hallstead.
478. Sephrona, Feb. 9, 1829, m. C. L. Hoyt.

244

Thomas H. Leete, son of Asahel (113), m. 1st, Phebe Collins, by whom he had four children. She died, and he m. 2d, widow Edna C. Ayers, by whom he had three children. She died March 24, 1847. He m. 3d, Nov., 1848, widow Roxaloma Hale. He died Nov. 17, 1863. She died Dec., 1881.

Mr. Leete was a man of energy and perseverance. In Dec., 1843, he removed from Washtenaw Co., Mich., to Clinton Co., Mich., then a wilderness. The winter was very severe, so that thousands of cattle died for want of food. The snow fell to a great depth and became crusted, so that it was impossible for cattle to forage. But Mr. Leete carried all his stock safely through the winter, and saved himself from pecuniary loss, by constantly felling forest trees, upon which his cattle could browse. And by his untiring energy he made his wilderness home to blossom like the rose.

479. Caroline, b.   m. Harvey Lippit.
480. Thomas,   d. aged 18.
481. John.   m. name unknown.
482. George,   left home to go to sea; never heard from.

483. William,   Nov. 29, 1837, m. Sarah A. Briggs.
484. Delia P.   Aug. 15, 1839.
485. Rebecca M., Mar. 22, 1843.

245

Epaphras Nott Leete. son of Asahel (113), m. Jan. 2, 1816, Harriet Wordsworth Thompson, born at Chatham, N. Y., June 27, 1794. He died Sept. 10, 1872.

486. Maria A.,   b. Oct.   8, 1816, m. Thos. L. Maxon.
487. Polly,   Mar.   4, 1818, m. F. Powers.
488. Rufus T.,   Aug.   9, 1819.
489. John,   April 7, 1821, m. M. Thompson.
490. Calvin D.,   Dec. 28, 1822, d. Aug. 7, 1843.
491. Esther Jennette,   Oct. 18, 1824, m. W. Simmons.
492. Wm. Nott,   Nov.   1, 1826.
493. Samuel Thompson, Nov. 26, 1828, m. C. R. Pomroy.
494. Benj. F.,   Feb. 25, 1831, m. Irene McNeil.
495. Dr. James M.,   Feb. 10, 1883, m. C. Harrison.
496. Gilbert M.,   Mar.   5, 1835, d. Oct. 25, 1839.
497. Harriet W.,   June   2, 1837, m. J. D. Sullivan.
498. Laura C.,   Aug. 23, 1839, d. June 20, 1852.

247 *Gould*

Lois Leete, dau. of Miles (114), m. Elmore Gould, of Milton, Vt.

    Harvey,   d.
    Aurora.
    Jerusha,   m. Gardner Wilbur.
    Henry.
    Amos.
    John.
    Zurilda.
    Louisa.

248

Russell Leete, son of Miles (114), m. Polly Kingsley, of Vermont. They resided at Williamstown, Mass., and removed to some of the western States.

    499. Eliza,   d. aged 20 years.
    500. Sophia.
    501. William.
    501½. Mason.

250

Harvey H. Leete, son of Miles (114), m. Dec. 6, 1820, Harriet Hotchkin, dau. of George and Sarah Hotchkin, of Amenia, Dutchess Co., N. Y. Residence, Smyrna, Chenango Co., N. Y.

    502. Geo. H., b. Oct. 8, 1821, m. Mary Jane Harwood.
    503. Harriet L.
    504. Henry A., Feb. 14, 1827, of Lebanon, Madison Co.,
    505. Almon H., Feb. 3, 1829.   [N. Y.
    506. Clarinda H.,   1832.
    507. Lydia E.,   1834, m. Reuben Geer.
    508. Mary M.,   1837.

252

Almon Leete, son of Miles (114), m. Sarah Beardsley, born Aug. 25, 1814, at Clintonville, N. Y.

510. Theodore, b. Jan. 11, 1838, d. Feb. 15, 1844.
511. Jane, July 23, 1844.
511½. Henry, Oct. 25, 1847.
512. Mary Florence.

253

John G. Leete, son of Miles (114), m. Amy Ketcham, of Chautauqua, N. Y. They moved, in 1851, to Michigan.

513. Lucy, m. —— Winters, of Plattsburgh, N. Y.
514. Elizabeth.

254

Henry Leete, son of Miles (114), Ruth Nichols Grover, dau. of Edmund and Harriet Grover. She died at Clintonville, N. Y., Dec. 4, 1840. He afterward removed to California. No children.

255 *Goodwin*

Roxanna Leete, dau. of Miles (114), m. James P. Goodwin, of Peru, Clinton Co., N. Y. They had a large family. They removed to Illinois in 1849, Winnebago Co.

    Henry N.
    Levi F.
    Moelendoff Orleff.
    Benjamin I.
    Loomis L.
    James Monroe.
    Cordelia M.

Martha A.
Mary E.
Abigail I.
Stephen D.
James H.
Another.

256   *Goodwin*

Wealthy Leete, dau. of Miles (114), m. Apollos Goodwin, of Peru, Clinton Co., N. Y. They removed, about 1839, to Winnebago Co., Illinois, Sugar River Precinct.

Miles.
Sylvia C.
Henry R.
Wesley I.
Guy F.
Theophilus V.
Mary P.
Earl.
Wealthy J.
Benjamin M.
Alexis O.

257   *Fitzgerald*

Elizabeth Leete, dau. of Miles (114), m. Richard Fitzgerald, of Burlington, Vermont.

Ellen E.

258

Amasa Leete, son of Absalom (116), m. April 27, 1801, Abigail Stone, dau. of Noah Stone and Martha Ludington, of Guilford, born April 19, 1774. He resided in Guilford, and became insane. He died, aged 43, Dec. 4, 1813. She died, aged 61, Oct. 2, 1835.

515. Rachel,   b. May 17, 1802, m. James Taylor.
516. Jordan,   June 25, 1803. drowned Aug. 25, 1807.
517. Rodolphus,   1805, died at sea, 1826. He fell from masthead of a whale ship.
518. Warren,   1808, d. Nov. 20, 1813.
519. Mary,   m. Geo. Field.
520. Oswell,   d. aged 18.

259

Linus Leete, son of Absalom (116), m. 1st, Betsey Dudley, dau. of Nathaniel Dudley and Abigail Chittenden, of Guilford, born Dec. 7, 1780. She died, aged 32, Jan. 15, 1813. He m. 2d, in 1813, Rhoda Fowler, dau. of Josiah Fowler and Rhoda Atkins, of Guilford, born Aug. 30, 1785. She died aged 79, Mar. 29, 1865. He lived in East Guilford and in Killingworth, and died, aged 84, Dec. 22, 1861.

521. William,   b. Mar. 10, 1800, m. Betsey Merritt.
522. Eliza,   Aug. 25, 1802, m. Joel Rice.
523. Polly,   Sept. 20, 1806. s.
524. Horace,   July 31, 1810, m. Lovina Booth.

525. Josiah Fowler,   Nov. 3, 1814, m. Sarah Butler.
526. Henrietta Jane,   Feb. 17, 1817, s.
527. Thaddeus Maltby,   June 3, 1819, m. Caroline Harvey.
528. Alonzo,   May 12, 1822, m. Barbara Hull.
529. Rhoda,   April 24, 1826, m. Julius Stone.

261

Absalom Leete, son of Absalom (116), m. Sally Pease, of Glastonbury, Conn., born in 1793. She died, aged 59, Aug. 14, 1852. He resided in Madison (East River), and died, aged 75, Nov. 25, 1857. He was a wheelwright.

530. Lucy Ann, b. Oct. 16, 1814, m. Austin Hull.
531. Harriet M., Jan. 3, 1816, s. insane, d. May 7,
532. George Warren, Mar. 11, 1819, m. Jane Buell. [1857.
533. David Edwin, Feb. 2, 1821, s. d. Feb. 9, 1855.
534. Anson Lewis, July 16, 1823, m. J. B. Norton.
535. Mary Jane, Nov. 9, 1825, s. d. Sept. 25, 1842.
536. Martha Emeline, Dec. 7, 1827, m. Sam'l N. DeFor-
537. Miriam Adelaide, July 5, 1836. [est.

264

Dr. Frederic Leete, son of Solomon (121), m. 1st, Lucy Moore, m. 2d, —— ——. Residence, New York City.

538. William Edwin, b. Nov. 25, 1811, m. Marcia Boardman.
539. Eveline E., m. Garwood Hinman.
540. Mary J., m. David Stevens.

266

William Leete, son of Solomon (121), m. Susan Humphrey. They resided in Green Co., N. Y., and in other places, and had 4 children; names not given.

267

Uriah Leete, son of Solomon (121), m. in 1815, Mary Ives, dau. of Timothy Ives, of Cambridge, Mass. Residence, Bingham, Potter Co., Pa.

541. Betsey E., b. Feb. 16, 1816, m. Samuel Chapman.
542. Horace, May 25, 1818, m. Ellen Wetherby.
543. Ralph, Esq., Jan. 12, 1823, m. Harriet E. Hand.
544. Timothy J., Feb. 11, 1829.
545. Sarah, April 11, 1833, m. W. C. Hood.
546. John R., Feb. 22, 1838.

268

Abner Leete, son of Solomon (121). m. Polly Remsen, of Cazenovia; residence, Bingham, Pa., and Alleghany Co., N. Y. He died in 1850; his wife in 1846.

547. Thomas Remsen, b.   1815.
548. Abner B.,   1817, d. 1848.
549. Uriah.
550. Julia.
551. B. Franklin.
552. Edwin.
553. Harriet.
554. Russell.   idiotic; d. aged 10.

269

Thomas Leete, son of Solomon (121), m. Aug. 20, 1817, Hannah Ives. Residence, Tioga Co., N. Y.

555. Perry,   b. May 18, 1818, d. April, 1852.
556. Albert D.,   Dec. 15, 1820, of Lynchburgh, Va.

274

James Leete, son of James (123), m. Zibeah Miller neé Richards, born Feb. 21, 1772. He died in Guilford, aged 61, Jan. 6, 1838. She died, aged 100 years and 7 days, Feb. 28, 1872.

557. Lewis,   m. Harriet Elliot.
558. Horace,   m. Sarah Kirkham.
559. John R.,   m. Mary A. Graves.
560. Samuel, b.   1811, s. d. May 23, 1836.
561. James,   m. Julia A. Plant.
562. William,   1819, s. d. Dec. 23, 1826.

275 *Bradley*

Juliana Leete, dau. of James (123), m. Benjamin Bradley, of Guilford, son of Simri Bradley and Ruth Hill, born Nov. 23, 1771. He died, aged 80, April 28, 1852. She died Jan. 29, 1840, aged 65.

    George,   b. Oct. 19, 1800, m. Sally Frisbie.
    Mary Ann,   Nov. 25, 1802, s. d. Oct. 7, 1871.
    Clarissa,   Dec. 17, 1804, m. Cyrus Churchill.
    Juliet,   July 20, 1807, m. John Dunn.
    Almira,   May 1, 1810.
    Benjamin,   May 6, 1812, m. Jane N. Tisdale.
    Samuel,   May 16, 1814, s. d. May 14, 1830.
    Joseph,   May 21, 1816, m. Jemima Weeks.

276

Peter Leete, son of James (123), m. July 26, 1809, Freelove Maynard. She died, aged 52, April 1, 1840. He died, aged 76, Mar. 18, 1864.

    563. Zibiah R.,   b. May 23, 1813, m. A. C. Scranton.
    564. Abigail W.,   Oct. 26, 1814, m. John Weld.
    565. Daniel M.,   June 9, 1816, m. C. Schoonmaker.
    566. George B.,   July 10, 1820. Went away.
    567. Joshua Goldsmith, May 1, 1824, m. Mary Parmelee.
    568. Isabella C.,   Feb. 19, 1833, m. Andrew J. Hull.
    Twin infants, born Feb. 19, died Mar. 9 and 19, 1812.

277

Daniel Brown Leete, son of Elijah (124), m. Mar. 13, 1821, Electa Fowler, dau. of James Fowler, of Killingworth, and Tempe Post, born June 3, 1801. She died, aged 74, Feb. 19, 1876. He died, aged 92, Aug. 6, 1873. In his prime he was a man of imposing physical proportions, standing six feet in his stockings. He was a custom house officer for thirty years, his duty being to board and inspect all incoming vessels. During the war of 1812 he boarded a West India vessel laden with rum, sugar and molasses, claiming to be bound to New Haven, to which place it was his duty to accompany it. When off New Haven, instead of running in, they kept on to Huntington, and attempted to bind or confine Mr. Leete, but by his commanding presence, physical force, and the use of his knife he kept them from their purpose. At Huntington they transferred their cargo to a sloop to go to New York, manned with two men and a boy. Mr. Leete boldly went aboard, and when near New York the crew in alarm escaped in their boat. He took the sloop in, it was condemned with its cargo and sold, and Mr. Leete received $1,000.

In 1860 his two sons, Jonathan and Elijah, were in the coasting trade between Guilford and New York, having for their only assistant on their sloop a Malay named Jack. When in the Sound off Norwalk, Mar. 15, 1860, they were both murdered and thrown into the sea. The bodies were never found, and Jack escaped the gallows because there was no legal proof of the murder.

569. Jonathan Fowler, b. Mar. 19, 1823, s. d. Mar. 15, 1860.
570. Temperance Post, Oct. 20, 1825, m. W. N. Wheeler.
571. Susan Brown, Sept. 20, 1829, m. H'y Botsford.
572. Elijah Jackson, July 9, 1832, s. d. Mar. 15, 1860.
573. Elizabeth, Feb. 22, 1838, m. Geo. C. Bowen.
574. Frances, Jan. 1844, d. May 17, 1845.

278

Samuel Leete, son of Elijah (124), m. Oct. 8, 1821, Julia A. Frisbie, dau. of Stephen Frisbie, of Guilford. He died, aged 62, Jan. 27, 1850. His widow died, aged 82, Dec. 3, 1877.

575. Juliana, b. Oct. 22, 1822, m. Geo. T. Newhall.
576. Maria, Sept. 2, 1824, m. Thomas Sault.
577. Sophia, July, 1826, d. July 31, 1829.
578. Sophia, May, 1828, d. Feb. 23, 1841.
579. Samuel R., May 16, 1830, m. Elizabeth Seward.
580. Clara, May, 1832.
581. Geo. A., Mar. 2, 1834, m. Emma ———.

279 *Stone*

Clarissa Leete, dau. of Elijah (124), m. Nov. 23, 1811, Bela Stone, of Guilford, son of Solomon Stone, of Guilford, and Elizabeth Griffing, of Branford, born Nov. 11, 1788. He died, aged 50, Feb. 19, 1839. She died, aged 78, April 13, 1868.

    Samuel Elmore, b. July 6, 1813, m. Abigail Spencer.
    Clarissa Jennette, June 30, 1815, s. d. Mar. 25, 1880.
    Charles Mortimer, Dec. 18, 1817, m. Ellen Benton.
    Elizabeth Leete, June 22, 1820, d. Nov. 6, 1835.
    Edward Griffing, July 26, 1826, d. Sept. 26, 1838.

280 *Moore*

Betsey Leete, dau. of Elijah (124), m. James H. Moore, of Bridgeport. She died without children, aged 74, April 12, 1867.

281

George Leete, son of Pharez (126), m. Jan., 1803, Experience Elliott, dau. of Col. John Elliott, of Guilford, and Experience Hempstead, of L. I., born Dec. 31, 1778. She died May 12, 1803. He m. 2d, Lucretia Sanford, and resided in North Haven, where he died, aged 44, Dec. 26, 1826.

    582. Mary Ann, b. April 1810, m. Henry Bradley.
    583. Lucretia, Sept. 1812, m. Wm. A. Peck.
    584. Eliza Experience, b. Feb. 15, 1815, m. Selah L. Dudley.
    585. Harvey B., b. Aug. 1817, m. Cynthia Clark.

282

Ruth Leete, dau. of Pharez (126), m. Nymphias Stacey. She died, aged 30, in 1815.

283

Anna Leete, dau. of Pharez (126), m. Dec. 13, 1820, Amos Leete (182).

285 *Tanner*

Flora Leete, dau. of Amos (131), m. Alexander Tanner.

286

Homer Leete, son of Amos (131), m. Emily Woodford.

287

Trumbull Leete, son of Amos (131), m. Harriet Lewis.

288 *Griffing*

Emily Leete, dau. of Amos (131), m. Rastus Griffing.

289 *Meacham*

Julia Leete, dau. of Amos (131), m. Horatio Meacham.

290

Sherman Leete, son of Amos (131), m. Sarah Truesdal.

290½

Geo. Leete, son of Amos (131), m. Jane Chew, of Brookfield, Ohio. He was a physician and lawyer. He died in 1843, aged 28.

595. Aurelia,	b.	1839, m. A. K. Viets.
596. Lamira,		1841, m. J. G. Clark.

291   *Stevens*

Elizabeth Leete, dau. of Jared (132), m. April 12, 1806, Amasa Stevens, son of Asa Stevens, of Killingworth. Residence, North Guilford. He died, aged 69, June 7, 1854. She died, aged 73, Jan. 29, 1859.

Alexander,	b. Feb. 16, 1807, m. Rachel Benton.
Wm. Alonzo,	Nov. 15, 1808, m. Emeline Beers.
Lucy Sophronia,	April 24, 1811, m. Wm. H. Evarts.
Andrew,	Aug. 20, 1813, m. Eliza Ann Ball.
Jas. Sylvester,	Feb. 4, 1816, m. Clarissa M. Evarts.
Lois,	April 24, 1819, m. Nathan Aldrich.
Sally Miriam,	July 5, 1821, m. Oliver Bailey.
Simeon,	Mar. 25, 1824, d. July 20, 1825.
Simeon Amasa,	May 24, 1827.

292

Jared Leete, son of Jared (132), m. 1st, Lydia Cook, of Wallingford, dau. of Titus Cook and Sarah Merriman, born April 1, 1778, who died, aged 70, Feb. 3, 1848. He m. 2d, Sally Thorpe Bunnell. She died Oct. 5, 1853. He died, aged 79, Feb. 25, 1866.

597. Simeon A.,	b. July	8, 1812, m. Delia Blake.
598. Clarissa,	May	16, 1815, m. Roswell Blake.
599. Lucina,	July	1817, m. Julius Blakeslee.
600. Parne,	Jan.	4, 1819, m. John Hotchkiss.

293   *Cook*

Ruth Leete, dau. of Jared (132). m. Titus Cook, of Wallingford, son of Titus Cook and Sarah Merriman, born Nov. 7, 1775.

Julia,	m. George Bull.
Lucretia,	m. —— Weber.
Jared R.	
Leverett,	m. —— Hotchkiss.
Andrew.	
Louisa,	m. Henry Lane.

294

Simeon Leete, son of Jared (132), m. April 4, 1827, Eliza Hotchkiss, dau. of Henry Hotchkiss, of Guilford, and Elizabeth Barnes, of East Haven, born Nov. 27, 1800. He died, aged 41, Feb. 23, 1833. She m. 2d, June 9, 1834, Edward Norton, of Guilford, and died, aged 77, Mar. 16, 1878.

601. William Henry, b. June 11, 1828, m. Sylvia Kelsey.

295   *Wilcox*

Lucy Leete, dau. of Jared (132), m. Oziel Wilcox, Feb. 20, 1826. They removed to Genesee.

296

James A. Leete, son of Jared (132), m. Dec. 20, 1818, Ursula Turner, who died, aged 34, Jan. 21, 1823, leaving one child. He m. 2d, Mar. 11, 1824, Hannah Cone, of Middletown, born Mar. 31, 1805. He died, aged 72, Aug. 18, 1868. She died Sept. 8, 1883.

601½. Elizabeth,   b. July 28, 1820, m. Henry Dowd.

602. James Andrew, b. Mar. 19, 1825, m. ——— McCarthy.
603. Ursula,   June 12, 1827, m. Daniel Webster.
604. Mary Ann,   July 7, 1829, m. Edwin Nettleton.
605. Sophronia,   July 20, 1831, m. Phineas L. Squire.
606. John Wm.,   Sept. 24, 1833, m. Julia ———
607. Sarah Amelia, May 6, 1837, m. Sherman E. Camp.
608. Susan Marilla, Nov. 1, 1840, m. H. H. Church.
609. Orton Roselle, July 30, 1844, m. Emma Stockwell.
610. Elsie Maria,   Oct. 30, 1848, m. Merwin Palmer.
611. Herbert Walter, July 25, 1852, d. June 26, 1853.

297

Alexander Leete, son of Jared (132), m. Feb. 23, 1820, Sally Coe. He resided in North Branford.

612. Eliza Ann, b. Dec., 1820, d. May 23, 1822.

301

Alonzo Leete, son of William (141), of Williamstown. Mass., m. Laura Hill, of Adams, Mass. He died Feb. 10, 1883, aged 66.

613. Laura A.,   b. Aug. 2, 1844, m. Tice F. Niles.
614. William A.,   July 5, 1846, m. Alice G. White.
614½. Joseph Franklin, April 26, 1848, of Oregon.
615. Oliver E.,   May 9, 1850, m. Jennie M. Parker.
616. Marietta,   Nov. 2, 1855, m. John B. Mowry.
617. Ida,   Nov. 1, 1858, m. Albert Moon.

302

Luther Leete, son of William (41), of Williamstown, m. Chloe Hill.

618. Cordelia E.,   b. Jan. 14, 1842.
619. Gilbert Luther.   Sept. 29, 1848, m. Amelia Rathburn.
620. Geo. Washington, April 13, 1850, m. Cynthia Ashley.
621. William Henry,   May 22, 1854, m. Mary Hawkes.
622. Chloe,   Oct. 25, 1855.
623. Mary Ellen,   April 17, 1858, m. Geo. H. Smith.
624. Joseph.   Dec. 12, 1859.

304

Samuel M. Leete, son of Edward A. (146), m. in 1818, Anna Atwood, born Sept. 17, 1798. She died, aged 83, Nov., 1881. He died, aged 87, Feb., 1882.

625. Abby Jane, b. Dec. 7, 1820, m. Edward E. Shipman.
626. Charles S.,   May 9, 1823, m. N. A. Richardson.
627. William A.,   Oct. 20, 1827, m. Helen Spear.
628. Sidney,   Dec. 14, 1830, d. 1835.
629. John M.,   Nov. 2, 1834, m. Sarah Tucker.
630. Rachel A.,   April 5, 1838, m. Elisha B. Cole.
631. Mary E.,   Jan. 1, 1842, m. D. Prentice Higgins.

305

John C. Leete, son of Edward A. (146), m. Dec. 25, 1822, Lydia Shipman. He died June 15, 1874. He resided in Chester, Conn.

632. Henry A., b. Sept. 30, 1823, d. Oct. 7, 1826.
633. Rachel A.,   Mar. 9, 1826, d. Mar. 13, 1848.
634. Harriet L.,   Mar. 5, 1828, m. Asahel Emmons.
635. Joseph H.,   July 27, 1833, m. Maria Post.
636. Eliza C.,   Mar. 5, 1835, m. Edward F. Parker.
637. Sarah J.,   Aug. 6, 1838, m. John Alexander.
638. Albert C.,   July 4, 1840, d. 1843.

308

Eliza A. Leete, dau. of Edward A. (146), m. about 1830, Joseph Haswell. She died, aged 32, in 1835.

309

Edward A. Leete, Jr., son of Edward A. (146), m. July 23, 1835, Mary W. Keller. He died, aged 69, Aug., 1874. Residence, Pittsburg.

639. Geo. Keller, b. July 9, 1836, m. Sarah B. Bryan.
640. Emma Catharine, Nov. 15, 1837, d. Mar. 13, 1839.
641. Allen Brown, Jan. 15, 1840.
642. John Brown, May 12, 1842, d. Dec. 13, 1874.
643. Elizabeth Connelly, Sept. 15, 1845.
644. Charles Boisel, Mar. 23, 1856.

310   *Young*

Eunice C. Leete, dau. of Edward A. (146), m. in 1842 Charles Young. She died, aged 75, Mar., 1883.

Charles. b. 1843, d. 1864.

311

George A. Leete, son of John Alfred (156), m. Nov. 25, 1845, Mary J. Hall, of Canandaigua, N. Y., born Mar. 6, 1821. She died, aged 26, April 20, 1847. He m. 2d, April 18, 1848, Elizabeth Farmer, of Concord, Mass., born July 1, 1829. He resided in Providence, and was President of the Providence and Worcester R. R. He died, aged 64, April 12, 1884.

645. Mary Jane, b. April 1, 1847, m. Charles B. Ford.
646. Geo. Farmer, b. Jan. 23, 1849, m. Hattie Remington.
647. Eliz. Julia, July 31, 1851, m. Edw'd W. Foster.
648. Wm. Alfred, Aug. 28, 1853, m. Sophia E. Rawson.
649. Chas. Henry, April 26, 1855, d. y.
650. Millicent H., May 31, 1856.
651. Edw'd Metcalf, July 30, 1857, d. y.
652. Sarah Louisa, Oct. 24, 1858.
653. Alex. Duncan, Nov. 3, 1861, Brown Univ., 1883.

Five others, born later, died young.

312 *Wilcox*

Cynthia E. Leete, dau. of John Alfred (156), m. June 6, 1844, Hiram Wilcox.

    Sarah Leete, b. Dec. 15, 1846, m. Chas. L. Day.
    Chas. E.,   April 4, 1851.

313

Ira V. Leete, son of John Alfred (156), m. April 8, 1849, Helena Ham.

    654. Kitty M., b. Dec. 28, 1849, m. Sachariah Adams.

314

Charles L. Leete, son of John Alfred (156), m. Nov. 12, 1856, Mary Benton. She died March 11, 1869. He m. 2d, Nov. 25, 1873, Martha Farmer, of Concord, Mass. Residence, West Bloomfield, N. Y.

    655. John Albert, b. Oct. 19, 1857.
    656. Chas. Benton, Feb. 21, 1860.
    657. William S.,   April 4, 1863, d. Jan. 31, 1864.
    658. Fannie,   Jan. 28, 1866, d. April 5, 1867.
    659. Mary,   Jan. 21, 1869, d. Aug. 30, 1869.

324

Henry William Leete, son of Edmund (165), m. Sept., 1824, Nancy A. Doolittle, dau. of Giles Doolittle and Amelia Thomas, of Wallingford, born Aug. 19, 1804. They resided in Wallingford, where he died, aged 43, Oct. 10, 1844.

    660. Sarah,   b. May 24, 1826, m. John Powers.
    661. Henry Edmund, Mar. 26, 1828, m. Cynthia Freeman
    662. George,   April 6, 1830, m. Mary Coughlan.

663. Elizabeth,   b. Oct. 9, 1833, m. William Smith.
664. Marietta Clarissa, July 19, 1836, m. A. K. Conklin.
665. Rachel Isabel,   Dec. 3, 1839.
666. Fanny Amelia,   July 30, 1842, m. John Anderson.

325

Benjamin C. Leete, son of Edmund (165), m. Dec. 25, 1824, Sarah Page, dau. of Joel Page and Mabel Smith, of Branford, born April 12, 1799. She died without children, aged 26, April 7, 1825. He m. 2d, July 30, 1827, Amanda Cook, dau. of John Cook and Lucy Cruttenden, of Guilford, born June 15, 1809. She died, aged 38, Oct. 30, 1847. He m. 3d, Mar. 19, 1849, Lurinda Palmer, dau. of Daniel Palmer, of Branford. She died, aged 30, Dec. 10, 1852, leaving one child. He m. 4th, May 29, 1853, Julia Kirkham, widow of Geo. A. Kirkham, of Guilford, b. July 9, 1805. He died, aged 79, Oct. 22, 1883.

666½. John Eugene,   b. June 30, 1828, d. July 18, 1829.
667. Daniel Sherwood, Sept. 11, 1829, m. Cornelia Norton.
667½. Benjamin,   Jan. 1, 1831, d. June 23, 1833.
668. Charity,   Sept. 15, 1832, m. Wm. Henry Lee.
669. Justin Orlando,   Sept. 2, 1834, m. Laura Jewell.
670. Sarah Page,   June 14, 1837, m. Peter A. Gauchet.
671. Mary Jane,   Dec. 16, 1838, m. Geo. L. Ross.
672. Douglas Merwin,   Jan. 6, 1841, m.
673. Emily Case,   May 31, 1843, m. Heman Pierson.
673½. Susan Amanda,   April 19, 1847, d. Mar. 13, 1868.

674. Adeline Augusta, Dec. 21, 1850, m. James Hurlbut.

326 *Fowler*

Fanny Minerva Leete, dau. of Edmund (165), m. April 13, 1829, Geo. Fowler, of Madison, son of Reuben Fowler and Adah Willard, born April 20, 1803. They resided in Madison, where he died, aged 80, April 25, 1883. No children.

327

Samuel W. Leete, son of Edmund (165), m. Emma J. Buell, dau. of Zephaniah Buell, of Clinton, and Clarissa Shelley, of Guilford, born April 17, 1812. He resided at Leete's Island, and died there, aged 67, Jan. 27, 1877. Farmer.

675. Judson Wyllis, b. Aug. 3, 1836, m. Rosetta Hill.

328 *Crampton*

Mary F. Leete, dau. of Edmund (165), m. Sept. 9, 1835, Russell Crampton, of Guilford, son of Wm. Crampton and Lydia Willard, of Madison, born April 6, 1815. They reside in Guilford and have no children.

329 *Field*

Eunice L. Leete, dau. of Edmund (165), m. Jan. 9, 1841, Philander Field, of Madison, son of John Field and Ruth Munger, born Jan. 16, 1816. Residence, Madison, and now Guilford.

Fanny Marilla, b. Oct. 15, 1841, m. Edgar Moodey.
Mary Jane, Mar. 31, 1844.
John Philander, May 27, 1849, m. Hattie Cook.
William Munger, April 26, 1853, m. Emma A. Cook.

330

Sidney W. Leete, son of Ambrose (167), m. Susan H. Atwater, of New Haven, dau. of Jeremiah Atwater and Mary Cutler, born Mar. 25, 1801. She died, aged 72, Mar. 26, 1873. He died, aged 33, Aug. 31, 1836. Residence, New Haven.

676. Charles Sidney, b. Mar. 20, 1826, m. Olivia M. Cannon.
677. Mary Catharine, May 1828, m. Wm. Dickerman.
677½. Ann M., 1830, d. Aug. 26, 1836.

331

Dea. Albert A. Leete, son of Ambrose (167), m. June 6, 1825, Betsey A. Parmelee, dau. of Dan Parmelee and Polly Linsley, of Fair Haven, born Dec. 23, 1805. She died Oct. 14, 1881, aged 76. He was chosen a deacon of the First Church in Guilford, May 3, 1832. Residence, Guilford. Has been an active member of the First Church sixty-two years. Farmer.

678. Mary Ann, b. Sept. 20, 1827, m. E. A. Leete (701).
679. Sidney Ward, April 7, 1833, m. Isabelle H. Clark.
680. John Fowler, May 1, 1838, d. Feb. 13, 1840.
681. Martha Elizabeth, June 4, 1841, m. Sam'l S. Parmelee.
682. Harriet Cornelia, April 3, 1848.

332 *Fowler*

Harriet Leete, dau. of Ambrose (167), m. Nov. 29, 1837, John E. Fowler, of Guilford, who died, aged 35, July 29, 1838. She m. 2d, May 24, 1846, Medad Holcomb, of Guilford, who died Oct. 14, 1858. No children.

333

Ambrose W. Leete, son of Ambrose (167), m. Feb. 5, 1840, Abigail M. Leete (698). They reside in Guilford. Farmer.

683. Sarah Ward, b. Nov. 5, 1841.
684. Lewis Butler, Oct. 13, 1844, m. Sarah E. Snow.
685. Emeline Spencer, Sept. 16, 1851.

335 *Parmelee*

Miranda C. Leete, dau. of Ambrose (167), m. as 2d wife, Capt. Hezekiah Parmelee, of Fair Haven. He was lost at sea. She died, aged 56, Aug., 1870.

Cath. Almira, b. Dec. 18, 1846, m. Wm. B. Parker.
Charles Dan, Feb. 8, 1849, m. Sarah Mallory.
Lizzie Miranda, Sept. 9, 1851, m. Dr. A. C. Benedict.

336

Charles F. Leete. son of Ambrose (167), m. Mar. 14, 1845, Martha Hubbard Wright Lay, dau. of Steuben Lay and Martha Wright, of Westbrook, born Oct. 5, 1821. They reside in Guilford and have no children. He was a representative of the town of Guilford in the Connecticut Legislature in 1872.

337

Dea. Edward L. Leete, son of Miner (169), m. April 29, 1833, Sylvia Fowler, dau. of Daniel Fowler and Lucy Chittenden, of North Guilford, born May 2, 1807. He was a farmer, residing at Leete's Island. Has been a deacon in the First Church of Guilford since Nov. 14, 1852. He formerly taught in the public schools of Guilford, has been a trustee of the Guilford Institute since the first year of its active work, and has twice been a representative of the town in the Connecticut Legislature, in 1854 and 1865.

[In business he was a practical farmer, cultivating his ancestral acres at Leete's Island with diligence and success. For the last two years of his life impaired health laid him aside from active work. During this interval he busied himself in collecting, arranging, and preparing for the press this volume, as a contribution to the history of his Family. He prosecuted the work with much enthusiasm and success, and left it substantially completed. He died of valvular disease of the heart, aged nearly 74 years, May 3, 1884.

He was a man of settled principles and strong convictions, careful in forming his opinions, but never swerving from the strict rule of right. He had the respect, esteem and confidence of all who associated with him, and all justly considered him a personal friend.—T.]

686. Edward Walter, b. May 28, 1834, m. Harriet Rogers.
687. Lucy Louisa, Aug. 11, 1839, m. Dwight Rogers.

338

Rufus N. Leete, son of Miner (169), m. Oct. 23, 1833, Sarah Bishop, dau. of Ezra S. Bishop and Abigail Norton of Guilford, born Sept. 18, 1812. He is a prosperous farmer at Leete's Island, and is an efficient member of the Board of Trustees of the Guilford Savings Bank.

688. Nancy Maria, b. Oct. 23, 1834, m. W. G. Bishop.
689. Richard Miner, Nov. 20, 1836, m. M. E. Norton.
690. Roger Calvin, Aug. 30, 1838, m. Helen A. Park.
691. Ellen Lucretia, Aug. 20, 1840.
692. Rufus Burton, June 22, 1843.
693. Margaret Elizabeth, Mar. 11, 1846.

339

Rev. Theodore A. Leete, son of Miner (169), m. Sept. 3, 1851, Mary C. White, dau. of William White and Lois Cooley of Longmeadow, Mass., born Sept. 23, 1821. He is a graduate of Yale College, 1839, and of Yale Theological Seminary. He was pastor of the First Church, in Windsor, Conn., from 1845 to 1859, and has since supplied other churches in Connecticut and Massachusetts. He now resides in Longmeadow, Mass.

694. Ella Louisa, b. Mar. 28, 1853, m. E. F. Chapman.
695. Rev. Wm. White, Oct. 11, 1854, m. S. E. Rockwell.
696. Theo. Woolsey, Nov. 4, 1856.

340

Dea. Calvin M. Leete, son of Miner (169), m. Feb. 7, 1866, Lucy M. Leete (705). He is a farmer, residing at Leete's Island, and was a representative of the town of Guilford to the General Assembly of Connecticut in 1856, 1862 and 1878.

697. Calvin Morris, b. Jan. 11, 1867.

342

Capt. Alvan Leete, son of Joel (172), m. Jan. 15, 1816, Rebecca, widow of William Butler and dau. of Isaac Palmer and Abigail Tyler of Branford, born Feb. 14, 1789. She died, aged 73, Jan. 16, 1862. He died, aged 91, July 6, 1882. He was for many years a successful teacher in the public schools of Guilford and other towns.

    698. Abigail Maria, b. Nov. 18, 1816, m. A. W. Leete, (333).
    699. Eliza Ann.   Mar. 3, 1818, m. C. Robbins.
    700. Isaac Palmer,   Mar. 9, 1821, m. Clarissa Foote.
    701. Edwin Alonzo,   Dec. 21, 1822, m. S. E. Hotchkiss.
    702. Marietta,   July 20, 1827, s. d. Jan. 18, 1877.

344

Morris A. Leete, son of Joel (172), m. Oct 25, 1820, Clarinda Graves, dau. of Milton Graves and Lucy Buell, of Madison, born Aug. 27, 1799. She died, aged 63, May 23, 1863. He was killed by a fall Dec. 23, 1864, aged 69. He was a blacksmith and resided in Guilford.

    703. Joel Morris.   b. Dec. 25, 1821, d. Oct. 7, 1838.
    704. Geo. Augustus,   May 4, 1824, d. Nov. 27, 1825.
    705. Lucy Maria,   June 2, 1827, m. C. M. Leete (340).
    706. Geo. Cornelius,   Sept. 17, 1829, m. Harriet Stebbins.
{ 707. Henry Walter,   Nov. 9, 1832, s. d. Feb. 26, 1852.
{ 708. Harvey Ward,   Nov. 9, 1832, m. C. Faulkner.
    709. Joseph Alvan,   Aug. 19, 1836, m. Orphana Hill.

345

Frederic W. Leete, son of Joel (172), m. Statira J. Fowler, dau. of Thomas Fowler and Lois Whedon, of North Branford, born Oct. 6, 1807. She died, aged 61, Oct. 8, 1868. He m. 2d, Nov. 16, 1869, Mary E. Dunn, dau. of John Dunn and Juliet Bradley, of Guilford, born Sept. 24, 1831. He died, aged 77, June 3, 1880, in Guilford.

710. Lucinda Jennette, b. June 29, 1829, m. John Norton.
711. Amelia Celestia,   June 19, 1831, m. H. W. Norton.
712. Wm. Gilbert,   Mar. 20, 1833, m. E. Scoville.
713. Nelson Fowler,   Oct. 26, 1839, m. Maria Dunn.
714. Charlotte Uretta,   Oct. 9, 1843, s. d. Dec. 6, 1876.
715. Joel Frederic,   Mar. 2, 1845, m. Clara Norton.

346

Allen N. Leete, son of Noah (173), m. April 9, 1835, Isabella S. Murden, of New York, born Feb. 9, 1814. He resided in New York, and was for some time engaged in the manufacture of fire-proof safes. He died, aged 87, May 19, 1880.

716. Allen Norton, b. Dec. 15, 1839, m. Emma Luckey.

348

Rev. Charles W. Leete, son of Noah (173), m. 1st, Jan. 16, 1822, Adeline Loomis, dau. of Jabez Loomis and Sarah Taylor, of Wisc., born May 5, 1801, by whom he had two children. She died Feb. 3, 1833. And 2d, Sophronia Stone. He was a Methodist clergyman and died in Verona, N. Y., aged 59, in 1858.

717. Charles Ward, b.   m. Eliza Willes.
718. Allen Norton,   April 24, 1825, m. Abigail Button.
719. Adeline,   June 20, 1836, s. d. Sept. 12, 1874.
720. Wilbur Fisk,   Feb. 8, 1839, m. A. Church.
721. Sophronia,   Sept. 9, 1842, m. E. G. Church.
722. Wm. Stone,   Feb. 20, 1845, m. Rose ———

349

Harley N. Leete, son of Noah (173), m. Betsey B. Leete (351). He resided in Verona, N. Y., and died there, aged 70, June, 1872.

723. Mary L.,   b. June 20, 1825.
724. Robert B.,   July 19, 1827, m. S. E. Cummings.
725. Sarah E.,   Jan. 15, 1832, m. Delos W. Gibbs.

350   *Hess*

Artemisia Leete, dau. of Noah (173), m. Solomon Hess.

351

Betsey B. Leete, dau. of Pelatiah (174), m. Harley N. Leete (349).

352   *Whaley*

Sophia M. Leete, dau. of Pelatiah (174), m. Justyn Whaley.

    Maria.
    Cecilia.
    Myrta.
    Harriet.

353   *Edes*

Myrta M. Leete, dau. of Pelatiah (174), m. Hiram Edes.

    Myrta.

354   *Pratt*

Amanda J. Leete, dau. of Pelatiah (174), m. Otis Pratt.

    Norton.   d.
    Sophia.
    } David.
    { Sarah.
    Harley.

356 *Benedict*

Sarah W. Leete, dau. of Pelatiah (174), m. Elias Benedict.

Lucy W.

357

Pelatiah W. Leete, son of Pelatiah (174), m. 1st, Elizabeth Fuller; 2d, Jennie Gardner.

358

Jonathan D. Leete, son of Anson (176), m. Lucy Hanchett. Residence, Westfield, Chautauqua Co., N. Y.

726. Sarah E. d.
727. Julia.

359

Simeon Leete, son of Anson (176), m. Harriet Weed, dau. of Alanson. Residence, Ellery, N. Y. He died, aged 80, Aug. 16, 1881. She died, aged 78, Oct. 6, 1881.

728. Mary Jane, m. Hiram Barnhart.
729. Henry C., m. Cordelia Gifford.
730. Alfred D., m. Ellen Strong.
731. Helen, m. Thomas Russell.
732. Ann Eliza, m. Eber Furlow.
733. George L., m. Georgiana ———.

360

Timothy Leete, son of Anson (176), m. Cynthia Kennedy, dau. of Thomas. He died, Dec. 17, 1836, aged 33. Residence, Poland, N. Y.

734. Martha, m. Andrew J. Hull.
735. Timothy, died in the army, aged 25, Oct. 12, 1862.

361

Lewis Leete, son of Anson (176), m. Mary Thumb, dau. of Nicholas Thumb, of Ellery, N. Y. He has resided at Hartfield, Kennedy, and Ellington, N. Y.

736. Mary,	m. J. Ellsworth.
737. Elizabeth,	m. Gilbert Strong, d.
738. Ophelia,	m. Harvey Mye.

362   *Herrick*

Eliza Leete, dau. of Anson (176), m. Nehemiah Herrick. He died about 1880. Residence, Dexterville.

Anson L.	
Cordelia.	
Emily.	
Maria,	d. 1881.

363   *Vorce*

Caroline Leete, dau. of Anson (176), m. William Vorce, of Ellery. About 1857 he was elected sheriff of Chautauqua County, and removed to Mayville, thence to Westfield.

Hiram,	killed in the late war, about 1862.
LaFayette,	died of consumption in 1862.
William,	died aged 12.

364   *Mason*

Maria Leete, dau. of Anson (176), m. John Mason, Esq., of Dewittville.

Julia Ann,	m. Simeon Brownell.
Aaron.	
John,	m. resides in Chicago.
George,	m. Harriet Brownell.

365

Franklin Leete, son of Anson (176), m. 1st, Sally Sumner, dau. of Darius Sumner. She died April 3, 1865, and he m. 2d, Louisa Jones, dau. of Festus Jones, of Ellery, N. Y. Residence, Chautauqua Point.

739. Sarah,	m. Charles Young.
740. Caroline,	m. D. H. Geddes.
741. Fayette G.,	m. Helen Olds.
742. Charles S.,	m. Lillie Haskins.
743. Martha,	s. d.
744. Emma C.	
745. Elsie E.	
746. Lizzie M.	
747. George E.	
748. Hattie L.	

366

William Leete, son of Anson (176), m. 1st, Dec. 27, 1840, Eliza Ann Strong, dau. of Gabriel Strong, of Collins, Erie Co., N. Y. She died, aged 30, Nov. 21, 1850. He m. 2d, Dec. 21, 1852, Harriet S. Belden, of Ellery. He resides at Point Chautauqua and has twice been treasurer of Chautauqua County.

749. Anson G.,	b. Feb. 10, 1844, m. A. Thompson.
750. Mary E.,	Feb. 25, 1854.
751. Willis D.,	Oct. 29, 1856.
752. George E.,	Sept. 18, 1862.
753. Eliza A.,	Mar. 23, 1866.

367 *Barnhart*

Mary Leete, dau. of Anson (176), m. Dec. 8, 1840, Henry W. Barnhart, of Chautauqua Co., N. Y., born Jan. 11, 1816. They resided in Chautauqua County until 1865, when they removed to Michigan. They now reside in Grand Rapids, Mich.

Rev. Clinton L., b. Sept. 1, 1842, m. Jennie Martin.
Willard, Sept. 16, 1844, m. Eliza Vickery.
Franklin, Nov. 19, 1846, m. F. Judson.
Oren H., Feb. 9, 1850, m. Carrie Cobb.
Charles, July 30, 1852, s. d. Sept., 1878.
Deloss, May, 1855, d. 1861.
Emma, 1857, d. 1861.
Ella, 1860, m. Wm. Judson.

This family has been very prosperous and noted for integrity as well as success. The mother of this family is said to be "a woman of such sweetness of disposition as never to have been known to make an enemy." "Her children arise up and call her blessed."

Rev. Clinton L., the eldest, is an eminent minister of the M. E. Church and Presiding Elder of the Ionia District, Mich. The other members of the family have made themselves wealthy by dealing in pine lands and pine lumber, etc.

368   Caldwell

Emeline W. Leete, dau. of Augustus (177), m. in 1839 Robert Caldwell. She died in 1875.

Alfred A., b. 1841, d. in Salisbury prison, 1863.

369

Matheson W. Leete, son of Augustus (177), of North East, Erie Co., Pa., m. Betsey Coombs. He died, aged 53, in 1863.

754. Wilson, b. April 1, 1845.
755. Frank, Nov. 1846.
756. John, 1853.

371 *Rogers*

Lydia Z. Leete, dau. of Augustus (177), m. in 1847 Zenas Rogers.

 Cora A., b. Feb. 29, 1860.

373 *McCord*

Amanda Leete, dau. of Simeon (178), m. Joseph McCord, of North East, Pa.

Hannah E., b.	1839, m. Geo. Selkrigg.
Simeon,	1841, m. Nancy Loomis.
Andrew,	1843, m. Anna Mary Tuttle.
Robert,	1845.
Eliza,	1847, m. S. T. Moorhead.
Nancy M.,	1849.
Anna,	1852, m. Geo. A. Hampson.
Joseph,	1856.
Susan M.,	1858.

374

Alfred N. Leete, son of Simeon (178), m. in 1852, Harriet S. Hampson. Farmer and fruit grower, Moorheadville, Pa.

757. Charles A.,	b.	1853, m E. Moorhead.
758. Cora Isabel,		1862.
759. Simeon,		1865.

375

Calvin Leete, son of Simeon (178), of Moorheadville, Pa., m. 1st, in 1844, Eleanor Elliot, who died in 1867. He m. 2d, in 1868, Emily Moorhead. Farmer and fruit grower.

760. Clarissa Matilda, b. 1845, m. J. C. Moorhead.
761. Georgiana E., 1849, m. T. S. Wagner.
762. Calvin E., 1851.
763. Elizabeth S., 1859.
764. J. Neely. 1866.

765. Rebecca Moorhead, 1869.

377   Moorhead

Matilda Leete, dau. of Simeon (178), m. in 1842, J. R. Moorhead, of Moorheadville, Pa.

Robert Simeon, b. 1846, d. 1846.
Jane McCreary, 1860, m. C. D. Shaver, 1883.
Adelle Naomi, 1862.
Susan Leete, 1865.

378   Elliot

Ann Leete, dau. of Simeon (178), m. in 1845, Plara Elliot. She died in 1867.

Albert H., b. 1847, m. Ida Jones.
Frank L., 1849, d. 1849.
Clara, 1851.
Elizabeth H., 1853.

381   Minor

Elizabeth Leete, dau. of Eli (180), m. Sept. 1, 1841, James Minor, of New Haven, son of Eastman Minor and Eunice Strong, of Woodbury, born Sept. 1, 1815. He died in the army Oct. 17, 1863. No children.

382   Walkley

Caroline A. Leete, dau. of Eli (180), m. Warren Walkley. They reside in Hartford.

Edward Leete, b. Sept. 25, 1854, m.
James Minor,   Sept. 23, 1856, s. d. Sept. 19, 1882.
Francis Sereno,   July 18, 1859, s. d. Oct. 1, 1882.
Richard Warren, Jan. 11, 1863.

383 and 384

Sereno F. Leete, son of Eli (180), has never married. He owns a place in Durham, Conn., and resides there. His sister Maria (384), keeps house for him. He has been a representative from the town of Durham in the Connecticut Legislature.

385

Wm. P. Leete, son of Amos (182), m. Oct. 16, 1844, Elizabeth Z. Goodrich, of Branford, born Oct. 16, 1826. He removed to Barre, Wis., about 1859.

766. Sherman Morris, b. Feb. 2, 1846, m. C. Sheriden.
767. Joseph Goodrich,   Aug. 22, 1847, m. Ellen Pitkin.
768. George Harvey,   May 31, 1849, m. Sarah Callahan.
769. Mary Elizabeth,   Nov. 24, 1851, s. d. Aug. 6, 1875.
770. Wm. Woodruff,   Sept. 28, 1853, m. Kate Collins.
771. Zaida Louisa,   Dec. 10, 1855, m. C. H. White.
772. Frank Elizur,   June 23, 1858, m. Z. E. Moran.
773. Charles Ward,   1864, s. d. Nov. 9, 1881.

386   Rose

Ruth Leete, dau. of Amos (182), m. as 2d wife, July, 1847, Alvan B. Rose, of Fair Haven. She died May 20, 1860. He died, aged 71, Oct. 14, 1881.

Elbertine Elvira,   s. d.
Anna Marietta, b. May 28, 1851, d. April 7, 1875.

387   *Hall*

Anna Leete, dau. of Amos (182), m. April 7, 1848, Samuel L. Hall She died July 29, 1861.

    Walter H.,   b. July 23, 1850.
    Emma E.,   Dec. 5, 1852.
    Mary A.,   Sept. 7, 1858.
    { Samuel,   July 29, 1861, d. Oct. 29, 1861.
    { Sarah,   July 29, 1861, d. Nov. 3, 1861.

388   *Benton*

Hannah W. Leete, dau. of Amos (182), m. as 2d wife, Jan. 1, 1855, Raphael W. Benton, of Guilford. He was killed in the war, aged 41, Sept. 25, 1862. She removed to Wisconsin.

    Wallace Leete,   b. June 19, 1856.
    Webster Augustus,   Dec. 25, 1860.

389

Amos H. Leete, son of Amos (182), m. Feb. 17, 1868, Sarah A. Way, of New Haven. Residence, Fair Haven and Baltimore.

    774. Wm. Clayton,   b. Aug., 1870.

390   *Hepburn*

Clarissa M. Leete, dau. of Harvey (184), of Fayetteville, N. C., m. Oct. 27, 1840, Dr. James C. Hepburn, and in 1841 entered upon missionary work, first at Singapore, then at Amoy, China, and since 1859 in Japan. She was the first missionary lady to enter the latter field.

    Samuel D.,   m. Clara E. Shaw.

He was born in Amoy, China, graduated at Princeton, N. J. Now resides in Japan, agent of a steamship company. Six others died young.

393

Col. Charles E. Leete, son of Harvey (184), m. Nov. 9, 1852, Sarah Louisa Hawley, born Aug. 13, 1826. She died Jan. 1, 1857. He died Jan. 30, 1867.

775. Frank Harvey, b. Aug. 13, 1853, d. April 29, 1857.
776. Louisa Arlena, May 6, 1855, missionary to Japan.

394

William J. Leete, son of Harvey (184), m. Dec. 12, 1850, Ann Pugh, of Texas, born Nov. 11, 1834. She died Nov. 5, 1872. He died Oct. 23, 1873.

777. Sarah Adriana, b. June 26, 1852, m. J. W. Ethridge.
778. James Pugh, Sept. 9, 1856, d. April 3, 1872.
779. Mary Isabella, Jan. 12, 1859, d. July 13, 1863.
780. Francis Harvey, Feb. 1, 1861, d. Nov. 30, 1866.
781. Charles William, Nov. 2, 1865.
782. John Henry, Mar. 20, 1869.

395

Isabella A. Leete, dau. of Harvey (184), is a missionary in Japan.

406

Benjamin Leete, son of Benjamin (199), m. 1842, Jane E. Richardson. Residence, Windsor, Vt.

783. Eunice, b. Jan., 1843, m. Charles Bliss.
784. Adelaide, Sept., 1844.
785. Philetta, April, 1846, m. Edward P. Marsh.
786. Jennie, June, 1849, m. Andrew Roy.
787. George W., Sept., 1851.
788. Flora, Aug., 1854, m. George Heath.

409   *Webber*

Susan Leete, dau. of Benjamin (199), m. Charles Webber.

412   *Leonard*

Philinda Leete, dau. of Benjamin (199), m. Franklin Leonard.

414   *Wilson*

Eunice Leete, dau. of Benjamin (199), m. Adam Wilson.

    Webster.
    James

415   *Ellis*

Maria Leete, dau. of James (201), m. Charles Ellis.

    James.
    Abby.

416   *Randall*

Jane Leete, dau. of James (201), m. Lewis W. Randall.

    Clara.
    Ella.
    another.

417

James Leete, son of James (201), m. Dec. 23, 1845, Lucy Ann Maynard. He resides in Claremont, N. H.

789. Eugene F.,   b. Dec. 11, 1846, m. Georgia Haynes.
790. Clarence M.,   Aug. 22, 1850, m. Minnie Ladd.
791. Wallace M.,   June 21, 1852, m. Madora A. Byron.
792. Nellie C.,   Feb. 5, 1860, d. Jan. 2, 1863.

419

Charles Leete, son of James (201), m. April 9, 1856, Frances A. Holden, of Billerica, Mass. He resides in Upton, Mass., now, but formerly lived in Roxbury, where all his children were born. Formerly he was a provision dealer, now a farmer.

793. Charles Frederic, b. Dec. 27, 1857.
794. Fanny Florence,   April 30, 1860, m. H. J. Seymour.
795. Wm. Augustus,   Aug. 15, 1863, d. Dec. 23, 1879.
796. Cora Gertrude,   Dec. 26, 1867.
797. Edith May,   Aug. 30, 1872.
798. Geo. Edward,   Jan. 9, 1875.

420

Edwin Leete, son of James (201), m. Fidelia Bliss and left no children.

421   *Royce*

Abby C. Leete, dau. of James (201), m. Carl Royce.

    Florence.

422   *Kidder*

Rhoda Leete, dau. of John (202), m. Hamden Kidder.

    Oscar.
    Olivia.
    Fanny.

423 *Marston*

Lucretia Leete, dau. of John (202), m. Elisha Marston.

    Frances.
    Jane.
    Jennette.
    Agnes.
    Ida.
    Frederic.

424

Frederic Leete, son of John (202), m. Susan Combs.

    799. Martha.
    800. Polly.
    801. Fanny.
    802. James.
    803. John.
    804. Willie.
    805. Charles.

425

John Leete, son of John (202), m. Sarah Green.

    806. Darwin.
    807. Duron.

426

Lemuel Leete, son of John (202), m. Mary Green.

    808. Nettie.
    809. George.

429

Dexter Leete, son of Ezra (210), m. Jane Bayne. He resides in Geneseo, Livingston Co., N. Y.

810.	James, b.	1841.
811.	William,	1846.
812.	Dexter,	1850.
813.	Lizzie,	1852.
814.	Sarah,	1854.
815.	Mary,	1859.

431

Ezra Leete, son of Ezra (210), has a wife and family in Ontario.

433

Reuben Leete, son of Reuben (211), m. May 10, 1852, Elvira L. Andrews.

816.	Mary Ann,	b. Nov. 21, 1853.
817.	Wm. Augustus,	Dec. 4, 1854, of Ryegate, Vt.
818.	Ella Elvira,	May 26, 1857, m. Harry Holton.
819.	Ada,	June 8, 1860, d. young.
820.	Nelson,	Jan. 30, 1863.
821.	Laura Lenora,	Aug. 26, 1865.

434

George W. Leete, son of Reuben (211), m. 1st, Nov. 24, 1848, Lucina Williamson. Residence, Castleton, P. Q., Canada. She died Dec. 26, 1863. He m. 2d, Dec. 23, 1868, Martha Addie Parker.

822. Seth Penn, b. April 26, 1851, m. C. Colwell.
823. Orpha Ada, Aug. 13, 1852, m. Wm. W. Minor.
824. Warren Reuben, Jan. 24, 1856, m. Sarah Olney.
825. Lynn T., May 9, 1858, stud'ng law, Montreal.
826. Eddy M., Sept. 11, 1860, m. Sadie Burbank.

827. Noel Mayo, Feb. 21, 1870.
828. Lely Lorne, Jan. 24, 1872.
829. Merrick Addie, Sept. 26, 1875.
830. Agnes Martha, July 7, 1882, d. March, or Apr., '84.

435   *Willey*

Clarissa Leete, dau. of Reuben (211), m. Wellington Willey, Oct. 7, 1840, and had four children. She died, Sept. 22, 1874, aged 51.

436

William Leete, son of Reuben (211), m. Sept. 25, 1848 Caroline Willey. He died at Acapulco, Mexico, May 21, 1852, aged 25.

437   *Barnum*

Belinda Leete, dau. of Reuben (211), m. Sept. 1, 1852, James H. Barnum. They reside at Brushton, N. Y.

    William, b. July 20, 1855, m. Bertha Eggleston.
    Jennie Early, Dec. 19, 1859, m. Chas. D. Baily.
                                    He is in Mexico.

438   *Willey*

Tapher Leete, dau. of Adam R. (214), m. Worcester Willey and had four children.

439   *Olney*

Rachel Leete, dau. of Adam R. (214), m. John Olney, and had three children.

440

Adam R. Leete, son of Adam R. (214), m. Flora Magoon. They reside in Shipton, P. Q., Canada.

831. Susan C.,   b. July 14, 1855.
832. Kenneth,   May 9, 1862.
833. Harley,   Feb. 6, 1864.

441   *Hall*

Chloe A. Leete, dau. of Adam R. (214), m. Moses W. Hall. They reside in Shipton, Canada, and have two children.

443

Adam R. Leete, son of David M. (215), m. Louise C. Gage. They reside in Claremont, N. H., and have no children.

444   *Denison*

Eleanor Leete, dau. of David M. (215), m. Avery Denison. Residence, Shipton.

Cora,   m. Nelson Philbrick.
Lillie.
Simeon Miner.
Inez Mary.
Arthur.

445

Asa Leete, son of Cyrus (216), m. Mary Morse. Residence, Shipton.

834. Maria.
835. Alice M.
836. Edmund N.

446   *Greer*

Phebe Leete, dau. of Cyrus (216), m. Avery Greer. They live in Jersey City.

447

Loren Leete, son of Cyrus (216), m. and had three children, and died in Illinois, Nov. 9, 1878.

448

Cyrus Leete, son of Cyrus (216), m. Dorothy B. Bohanan. They resided in Claremont, N. H. Removed to Danville, P. Q.

837. Nellie A.
838. Bertha A.

449

Henry Leete, son of Cyrus (216), m. Nov. 4, 1862, Sarah Leavitt, of Eaton, P. Q., Canada, born July 2, 1839. They reside in Williston, Vt.

839. Celia O.,   b. Oct.   6, 1863.
840. Lillie M.,   May   2, 1866.
841. Charles M.,   June 18, 1868.
842. Ida B.,   May   6, 1872.
843. Gertie P.,   May   7, 1874.
844. George O.,   Mar. 15, 1876.
845. Edith G.,   Feb. 24, 1881.

450

Timothy Leete, son of Alvah (217). m. May 17, 1853, Mary Ann Mahaffy, born May 19, 1834. They reside in Shipton, P. Q., Canada, where he has been Town Clerk and Clerk of the Court for more than twenty-five years. He stands high in the Masonic Order in Canada.

846. Sarah Elizabeth,	b. Jan.	23, 1855, d. Mar. 16, 1856.
847. Chas. Edward,	Feb.	3, 1857, m. L. M. Lee.
848. George Isaac,	Sept.	19, 1858, d. June 2, 1876.
849. Hollis Oscar,	Mar.	27, 1860.
850. Nelson Eugene,	Oct.	27, 1863, d. July 5, 1864.
851. Cora Ada,	June	13, 1865.
852. Melina Emeline,	April	13, 1867.
853. Norman Edgar,	May	9, 1868.
854. Mary Ella,	Mar.	26, 1870.
855. Frederic Arthur,	May	9, 1873, d. May 9, 1876.
856. John Albert,	Aug.	23, 1875, d. Feb. 13, 1876.
857. Frank Ernest,	Jan.	23, 1879, d. Feb. 3, 1881.

451 *Adams*

Sarah M. Leete, dau. of Alvah (217), m. William Adams and had six children.

452

James Leete, son of Alvah (217), m. in 1860, Maria Doyle. Resides in Nevada.

858. Sarah E.
859. Stephen O.
860. Levi.
861. Mahala.

453

John Leete, son of Alvah (217), m. in 1858, Margaret A. Green. He died in 1872. She died in 1875.

862. Mary Annis,   d. in 1883.
863. Wm. Aylmer.
864. Timothy.
865. Ulysses G.
866. Hattie.

454

Simeon Leete, son of Alvah (217), m. in 1863, Margaret A. Andrews.

867. Arthur.
868. Clinton.
869. Arnold.
870. Fred.
871. Frank.

454½

Hiram Leete, son of Alvah (217), m. in 1872, Mary Dickey. He resides in Shipton, P. Q., in the house that his grandfather, Levi Leete, built in 1807, supposed to be the oldest inhabitable house in Shipton.

872. Edith.
873. Eva.
874. Winnie.
875. infant.

455   *Kenerson*

Abigail Leete, dau. of Hiram (218), m. Josiah Kenerson, of Barnet, Vt.

456

Levi Leete, son of Hiram (218), was killed in the first battle before Richmond. He was a sharp shooter. He left a wife and one son.

876. Levi.

457

Freeman Leete, son of Hiram (218), m. in Massachusetts and has four or five children.

458   *King*

Betsey Leete, dau. of Dea. Nathaniel (224), m. April 17, 1821, Joseph King. She died April, 1870.

    Martha.
    Mary.
    George.
    Dwight.
    Frank.
    Charles.

459

Horace Leete, son of Dea. Nathaniel (224), m. April 11, 1844, Elizabeth Caul. He lived in Freedom, Ohio, and died there in 1874. He had three children.

460

Chauncey Leete, son of Dea. Nathaniel (224), m. July, 1832, Mary Ward. He resides at West Stockbridge, Mass.

    877. Chauncey W.
    878. Sarah E.,   m. Wm. H. Edwards.

461   *Woodruff*

Sophia Leete, dau. of Dea. Nathaniel (224), m. 1st, Feb., 1831, Ashman Benedict; 2d, June, 1834, Harvey Woodruff. She died June 16, 1836, and left no children.

462 *Beebe*

Clarinda Leete, dau. of Dea. Nathaniel (224), m. Aug., 1846, Myron M. Beebe. She died Feb. 25, 1850.

  Hattie,   now of Rockville, Wis.

463 *Dudley*

Sarah Leete, dau. of Dea. Nathaniel (224), m. June 22, 1837, Charles Dudley. They live in Freedom, Ohio.

  Charles,   a graduate of Ann Arbor College, Mich.
  Plyman,   a graduate of Ann Arbor College, Mich.
  Willie.
  Frank.

464 *Salls*

Edna Leete, dau. of Dea. Nathaniel (224), m. June 3, 1841, Calvin Salls. She died without children, aged 23, June 14, 1842.

465 *Clark*

Olive Leete, dau. of Dea. Nathaniel (224), m. Dec. 28, 1842, John C. Clark, son of Rev. Azariah Clark, of Canaan Four Corners, N. Y.

  William,   m.
  Mary.
  Louisa,   m. W. H. Tinsley.

466 *Loper*

Lucy Leete, dau. of Abraham (227), m. Daniel Loper and settled in Genesee Co., N. Y.

467

Dr. Albert E. Leete, son of Eber (233), m. Catharine Palen and resided in Romeo, Mich. A practicing physician.

879. Clarinda,	b. Oct. 7, 1832, m. Henry Stephens.
880. Clarence P.,	Sept. 28, 1834, m.
881. Hannah,	Nov. 2, 1835.
882. James Edgar,	Mar. 10, 1838, m.
883. Rufus Palen,	June 3, 1842, d. Aug. 20, 1844.
884. Harriet P.,	Sept. 20, 1844.
885. Hallet,	Mar. 16, 1848, d. in the army, aged 16.

468   *Burton*

Clarinda Leete, dau. of Eber (233), m. June 25, 1825, B. K. Burton, of Amenia, N. Y. She died, aged 26, July 30, 1830.

Walter,	b.	1826, d. y.
Harriet Gale,		1828.
Albert E.,		1830, m. Mary McCarty.

470

Edgar J. Leete, Esq., son of Eber (233), has never married. He was for many years a lawyer practicing in New York. He now resides in Bayonne, N. J.

471

J. Sayre Leete, son of Harvey (238), m. Feb. 10, 1860, and removed to one of the Western States, where he died in 1874.

472

Asahel Leete, son of Noah (243), m. May 2, 1839, Emeline Grace Fowler, born Aug. 12, 1820. He enlisted in the army as a musician and died at West Point, Ky., Nov. 24, 1861.

    886. Franklin Marcellus, b. Dec. 26, 1841.
    887. Noah Arminius,   June 8, 1846.
    888. Mary Eliza,   Sept. 30, 1850, m. T. H. Fitch.

473   *Fenner*

Harriet S. Leete, dau. of Noah (243), m. Jan. 28, 1836, Alexander H. Fenner, born Feb. 16, 1811. He died, Aug. 9, 1850, aged 39.

    Olive M.,   b. Aug. 10, 1838, m. ―――― Wilcox.
    Orlando M.,   April 27, 1841, d. Jan. 17, 1845.

474   *Fenner*

Lucretia Leete, dau. of Noah (243), m. Feb. 22, 1839, Bela Fenner, born May 25, 1814.

    Emma A.,   b. Aug. 15, 1840.
    Albert L.,   Sept. 22, 1842.
    Weltha J.,   Nov. 5, 1844.
    Irving S.,   Oct. 26, 1846.
    Willis N.,   Jan. 1, 1855.

475   *Jackson*

Weltha Leete, dau. of Noah (243), m. Harlow Jackson, of Jennisonville, Mich.

476   *Morley*

Mary Ann Leete, dau. of Noah (243), m. Butler Morley, of Grand Rapids, Mich.

477   *Hallstead*

Martha Leete, dau. of Noah (243), m. May 17, 1849, Jesse D. Hallstead, of Chili, N. Y. He died, aged 38, Nov. 27, 1861.

    Hiram,   b. Jan. 13, 1856, d. Feb. 28, 1856.
    Mary A.,   Sept. 16, 1859.

478   *Hoyt*

Sophronia Leete, dau. of Noah (243), m. April 20, 1847, C. L. Hoyt.

    Ella D., b. June 6, 1855, d. July 25, 1864.
    Flora J., Feb. 4, 1857.

479   *Lippit*

Caroline Leete, dau. of Thos. H. (244), m. Harvey Lippit and moved to Wisconsin.

481

John Leete, son of Thos. H. (244), m., name of wife unknown. He died at the age of 24, leaving a son.

    John T.,   reported dead in 1862.

483

William Leete, son of Thos. H. (244), m. Jan. 1, 1855, Sarah A. Briggs. She died 1878. He died, Nov. 27, 1881, aged 43.

    890. Frances L., b. Dec. 25, 1856, d. April 15, 1860.
    891. Jennie M , June 27, 1859, d. Sept. 18, 1877.
    892. Willie A., Feb. 20, 1862, of Ovid, Mich.
    893. George E., April 24, 1866, of Ovid, Mich.
    894. Herbert D., Feb. 17, 1873, adopted by Mrs. Willey.
    895. Freddie R., Aug. 16, 1875, adopted by Mrs. Peterson.

484

Delia P. Leete, dau. of Thos. H. (244), m.

485

Rebecca M. Leete, dau. of Thos. H. (244), m.

486

Maria A. Leete, dau. of Epaphras Nott (245), m. Feb. 20, 1838, Thomas M. Mason. She died Apr. 25, 1846, leaving one daughter, name unknown.

487 *Powers*

Polly Leete, dau. of Epaphras Nott (245), m. Oct. 21, 1840, H. Freeman Powers. He died in military hospital during the late war. Two children, a son and daughter.

488

Rufus T. Leete, son of Epaphras Nott (245), is unmarried.

489

John Leete, son of Epaphras Nott (245), m. Mar. 7, 1844, Maria Thompson.

 896. Harriet R., b. Sept. 8, 1846, m. Edward Wilson.
 897. Orphia J., Sept. 20, 1851.
 898. Laura M., June 16, 1853, d. Nov. 23, 1866.

491 *Simmons*

Esther Jennette Leete, dau of Epaphras Nott (245), m. Apr. 28, 1864, Walter Simmons.

 Annie Laura, b. Aug. 23, 1865.
 Walter L., Jan. 23, 1867.

492

Wm. Nott Leete, son of Epaphras Nott (245), is unmarried.

493

Samuel Thompson Leete, son of Epaphras Nott (245), m. Aug. 22, 1855, Cynthia R. Pomroy.

494

Benjamin F. Leete, son of Epaphras Nott (245), m. Nov. 27, 1861, Irene McNeil.

495

Dr. James M. Leete, son of Epaphras Nott (245), m. June 28, 1871, Cordelia Harrison, dau. of James and Mary Louisa Harrison, born Aug. 14, 1839.

 899. Louisa, b. Jan. 10, 1874.
 900. Clara, April 30, 1876.

Received the degree of M. D. from the University of Pennsylvania, in 1861. Was Resident Physician in Blockley Hospital for two years. Was commissioned successively as Assistant Surgeon, Surgeon, and Medical Director in the army. He was in ten battles in the Shenandoah Valley and on recommendation of General Crook was brevetted Lieutenant-Colonel "for gallant and meritorious services during the engagements in West Virginia and the Shenandoah Valley." He was afterwards commissioned as Medical Director of the 20th Army Corps under Gen. W. T. Sherman, serving in this capacity till the close of the war. In September, 1865, he located himself in St. Louis, Mo., and entered upon the practice of medicine.

497

Harriet W. Leete, dau. of Epaphras Nott (245), m. John D. Sullivan. They have two children, a son and daughter.

502

George H. Leete, son of Harvey H. (250), m. Dec. 14, 1848, Mary Jane Harwood, born Aug. 13, 1824.

513

Lucy Leete, dau. of John G. (253), m. ———— Winters, of Plattsburgh, N. Y.

515 *Taylor*

Rachel Leete, dau. of Amasa (258), m. Nov. 24, 1822, James Taylor, and lived in New York. She became insane and died in North Madison, July, 1863, aged 61.

    Mary Jane, b. 1834, m. Henry Goldsmith and died without children Sept. 9, 1874.

519 *Field*

Mary Leete, dau. of Amasa (258), m. Aug. 29, 1830, George Field, of Madison, Conn., son of John Field and Ruth Munger, born 1800. He died, aged 63, Oct. 27, 1863.

    Oswell Warren, b. Dec. 4, 1830, d. May, 1849.
    Rodolphus Leete, July 4, 1832, m. Mary S. Way.
    Eliza, Feb. 6, 1834, m. David Atwater.
    Geo. Florentine, April 14, 1837, drow'd Dec. 19, '65.
    Martha Jane, Dec. 27, 1838, m. Capt. G. W. Caldwell.
    Mary, Oct. 25, 1841, m. 1st Fred'k Snow, 2d, Nathan Lane.

521

William Leete, son of Linus (529), m. Betsey Merritt. Residence, Waterbury, Vt. They had two children who died young. He married a second wife, widow Wealthy Blossom. He died aged 74, Oct., 1874.

522

Eliza Leete, dau. of Linus (259), m. Joel Rice, of New Haven. One child who died young. She died, aged 36, Sept., 1838.

524

Horace Leete, son of Linus (259), m. Lovina Booth. He died, aged 39, July 29, 1849. She died in 1875. Two children who died young.

525

Josiah F. Leete, son of Linus (259), m. May 12, 1850, Sarah Butler, of Wallingford, Conn., Jan. 29, 1831. Residence, Killingworth.

   901. Sarah Adella, b. April 20, 1852, m. Jacob Lane.
   902. Cherilla Eliza,   Sept. 26, 1854.
   903. Eugenia Horatia, Jan. 26, 1858, m. A. E. Perkins
   904. Horace Albro,   Mar. 17, 1861.
   905. Irwin Josiah,   Aug. 26, 1864.
   906. Betsey Jane,   May 30, 1868.
   907. Minnie,   May 20, 1872.

527

Thaddeus M. Leete, son of Linus (259), m. Sept. 30, 1849, Caroline Harvey, of Durham, born in Haddam, Sept. 30, 1826. Residence, first in Killingworth, since 1861, at East River, Madison.

   908. Wm. Harvey, b. June 30, 1850, d. Sept. 22, 1852.
   909. Emma Lucretia, Feb. 27, 1852.
   910. Mary Elizabeth, Aug. 16, 1853, m. R. L. Penny, Esq.
   911. Carrie Estella,   Sept. 29, 1855.
   912. Harriet Gertrude, Oct. 7, 1858.
   913. Alice Josephine, Aug. 13, 1860, m. Aug. 28, 1862.
   914. Fred'c Thaddeus, Jan. 3, 1865.

528

Alonzo Leete, son of Linus (259), m. 1st, Barbara Hull, who died, aged 49, Nov. 3, 1870. He m. 2d, Jan. 1, 1871, Sarah Abbey. He died, aged 54, Jan. 24, 1876.

915. Barbara E.,   b. Aug.,   1871, d. Feb. 11, 1875.
916. Bertha,   July,   1875.

529   *Stone*

Rhoda Leete, dau. of Linus (259), m. May 19, 1846, Julius Stone, of Killingworth, born Aug. 21, 1801. He died Jan. 20, 1871.

Julius,   b. May,   1847.
Olive Ann,   1854, m. E. F. Chittenden.
Irene Victoria,   Jan.,   1859.

530   *Hull*

Lucy Ann Leete, dau. of Absalom (261), m. in 1834, Austin Hull, of Clinton, Conn. Residence, Fair Haven. Children all born in Clinton.

Andrew Wesley, b. Feb. 3, 1835, m. A. Ludington.
Elizabeth Sarah,   Aug. 28, 1837, m. Wm. Walker.
Maronette Pease,   Feb. 18, 1840, m. Henry Lines.
Ellen Brown,   May 7, 1842, m. J. A. Bartholomew.

532

Geo. W. Leete, son of Absalom (261), m. 1st, Jane E. Buell, of Clinton, Conn., born Nov., 1823. He m. 2d, May 11, 1857, Emma J. Haight. Residence, Pleasant Grove, Cal. Emma died, aged 56, Apr. 16, 1878. He died, aged 62, Jan. 26, 1881.

917. George M.,   b. Oct.,   1847, d. Dec. 31, 1851.
918. Harriet Sophia,   April,   1844, m. W. Jacobs.
919. Christina Isabel,   July,   1849, m. Thomas Collins.

534

Anson L. Leete, son of Absalom (261), m. Jan. 11, 1846, Jennette B. Norton, dau. of Harry H. Norton and Diantha A. Norton, of Madison, born June 23, 1824. Residence, Madison, East River. He is a timber merchant.

   920. Mary Jane,   b. April 8, 1847, d. Mar. 27, 1849.
   921. Mattie Jennette,   Sept. 19, 1848, m. C. S. Woodhull.
   922. Sarah Talcott,   July 13, 1852, d. Sept. 7, 1857.
   923. Anna Eugenia,   June 19, 1859.

536   *DeForest*

Martha E. Leete, dau. of Absalom (261), m. July 14, 1850, Samuel N. DeForest, born near Rochester, N. Y., Nov. 24, 1828. They resided first in Madison but removed about 1860 to New Canaan, Conn., where they now reside.

   Mary Adelaide, b. Sept. 3, 1851, m. John Bishop.
   David Woolsey,   June 26, 1856, m. Nettie Lines.
   Geo. Milton,   Mar. 2, 1859, m. Josephine Sarls.
   John Lincoln,   May 9, 1861, m. Sarah Bishop.
   Elizabeth,   Sept. 18, 1863, m. Chas. Sammis.
   Charles Stanley,   Mar. 8, 1865.
   Clarence Leete,   Mar. 15, 1869.

538

Wm. E. Leete, son of Dr. Frederic (264), m. Feb. 28, 1854, Marcia A. Boardman. He is a lawyer in Coxsackie, N. Y.

   924. Mary S.,   b. Jan. 21, 1858, d. Dec. 2, 1861.
   925. William B.,   Aug. 9, 1860.
   926. Charles,   June 4, 1865, d. Dec. 13, 1865.

539   *Hinman*

Elizabeth E. Leete, dau. of Dr. Frederic (264), m. Garwood Hinman and had one child who died young. She died Apr., 1836.

540   *Stevens*

Mary J. Leete, dau. of Dr. Frederic (264), m. Oct. 11, 1842, David Stevens. She died Dec. 29, 1848.

David B.,	b.	1845, d. Jan., 1881.
William,		1847, d. 1851.

541   *Chapman*

Betsey E. Leete, dau. of Uriah (267), m. Samuel Chapman.

542

Horace Leete, son of Uriah (267), m. Feb., 1851, Ellen Wetherby. He is a merchant of Portsmouth, Ohio.

927. Mary Ives,   b. Oct. 11, 1855.
928. Adah.
929. a son.

543

Ralph Leete, Esq., son of Uriah (267), m. Nov. 24, 1848, Harriet E. Hand, born in England. She died in 1879. He is a lawyer of Ironton, Ohio, and has been a member of the Ohio Legislature.

930. Wm. Hand,   b. Sept. 12, 1850.
931. Edith Ives,   Oct. 12, 1853, m. John Hamilton.
932. Frederic,   1860.
933. Lizzie,   1868.
934. Ralph Herman,   1872.

545

Sarah Leete, dau. of Uriah (267), m. W. C. Hood.

557

Lewis Leete, son of James (274), m. Oct. 12, 1823, Harriet Elliot, dau. of Reuben Elliot and Grace Fairchild, of Guilford, born Apr. 22, 1803. They removed to Philadelphia. She died Aug. 17, 1843.

935. Elizabeth Heaton, b. Sept. 30, 1824, m. J. S. Strathers.
936. Ellen A., July 16, 1826, s. d. June 15, 1848.
937. Mary Chittenden, July 27, 1829, m. C. W. Otto.
938. Lewis Elliot, 1833, d. April 29, 1853.

558

Horace Leete, son of James (274), m. Sarah A. Kirkham, dau. of Bedad Kirkham and Ruth Redfield, of Guilford, born Feb. 9, 1820. He died June 25, 1872.

939. Sarah Amelia, b. April 9, 1838, m. C. W. Bradley.
940. Harriet Elliot, Feb. 22, 1840, m. E Eldridge.

559

John R. Leete, son of James (274), m. Mary Ann Graves, dau. of Ambrose Graves and Nancy Hopson, of Guilford, born Nov. 15, 1809. He died, aged 26, in the West Indies, Dec. 8, 1834.

941. Mary Ann, b.
942. John R., Jan. 23, 1834, m. Susan T. Rowe.

561

James Leete, son of James (274), m. Aug. 6, 1839, Julia A. Plant, of Branford. Residence, Brooklyn, N. Y., and Summit, Pa. They have three children.

943.
944.
945.

563 *Scranton*

Zibiah R. Leete, dau. of Peter (276), m. Anson C. Scranton, son of Russell Scranton and Abigail Maynard, of Guilford, born Mar. 18, 1810. Residence, Guilford and Fair Haven. She died, aged 63, Jan. 5, 1877. He m. 2d, widow of John Smith.

Frances Maria,   b. Aug. 23, 1834, m. Charles Jones.
Samuel Wilbur,   June 6, 1836.
Mary Louisa,   April 1, 1838, m. S. L. Beach.
James Andrew,   April 19, 1840, m. J. C. Edwards.
Freelove Augusta,   Mar. 4, 1842, m. R. H. Rich.
George Leete,   June 24, 1844.
Jno. Hayden Kent,   May 23, 1846, m. M. A. Connor

564   Weld

Abigail W. Leete, dau. of Peter (276), m. Oct. 1, 1838, John Weld, son of Edmund Weld, of Guilford, and Mercy Nettleton, of Killingworth, born Sept. 25, 1813. Residence, Fair Haven.

John Arthur, b. Nov.   1842.
Edward Leete,   1844, m. Emma C. Graves.

565

Daniel Leete, son of Peter (276), m. Catharine Schoonmaker. Resides in Kingston, N. Y. Has had three children who all died young.

567

Joshua G. Leete, son of Peter (276), m. Oct. 3, 1847, Mary Parmelee, dau. of Geo. Parmelee and Clarissa Griswold, of Guilford, born Aug. 14, 1828. Residence, Fair Haven. She died, aged 50, Dec., 1878.

946. Josephine Clarissa, b. Sept. 26, 1848, m. E. D. Smith.
947. Geo. Maynard,   Sept. 4, 1851, d. Oct., 1881.
948. Frank Griswold,   Sept. 7, 1853, m. R. A. Slawson.
949. Edgar Clayton,   Sept. 30, 1855, m. M. E. Crane.
950. Wilbur Scranton,   Feb. 27, 1867.

568   Hull

Isabella C. Leete, dau. of Peter (276), m. in 1852, Andrew J. Hull, of New Haven.

Frank Eugene, b. Aug. 23, 1856, m. Jennie L. Frost.
Alice Isabella,   May 28, 1861, m. J. C. Bradley, Jr.

570   *Wheeler*

Temperance P. Leete, dau. of Daniel B. (277), m. in 1857, Newton Wheeler, son of Newton Wheeler, of New Haven. She died, without children, Jan. 29, 1868, aged 42.

571   *Botsford*

Susan B. Leete, dau. of Daniel B. (277), m. Apr. 18, 1866, Henry Botsford, of Branford. Two children.

573   *Bowen*

Elizabeth F. Leete, dau. of Daniel B. (277), m. Feb. 10, 1864, George C. Bowen, of Guilford.

    James Lewis,   b. Oct. 3, 1867.
    Benjamin L.,   Nov. 8, 1869.
    Edward Mallory,   Nov. 29, 1871.
    and two others,   d. young.

575   *Newhall*

Juliana Leete, dau. of Samuel (278), m. May 29, 1844, George T. Newhall, son of Merrit Newhall, of New Haven. Carriage maker.

    Harriet Atwood,   m. G. A. Reynolds.
    George Thompson.
    Thomas Winthrop.
    Ida Imogene.
    Clifford Eugene.
    Theodore Valentine,   aged 4, drowned July 2, 1868.
    Julia Adele.

576   *Sault*

Maria Leete, dau. of Samuel (278), m. Thomas Sault. They had no children.

579

Samuel R. Leete, son of Samuel (278). m. May 1, 1856, Elizabeth S. Seward, dau. of Samuel L. Seward, of Guilford, and Huldah Sanford, of Saybrook, born May 31, 1833.

951. Samuel Alfred, b. Mar. 26, 1865, d. July 31, 1866.
952. Maria Sault, June 4, 1867.
953. Mary Elizabeth, May 29, 1874, d. July 29, 1876.

581

George A. Leete, son of Samuel (278), m. Emma ———. He died in New Haven, aged 35, Nov. 3, 1869, leaving a daughter.

954. Emma.

582 *Bradley*

Mary Ann Leete, dau. of George (281), m. Henry Bradley.

583 *Peck*

Lucretia Leete, dau. of George (281), m. Wm. A. Peck.

584 *Dudley*

Eliza A. Leete, dau. of George (281), m. Selah L. Dudley, of North Guilford, afterward of San Francisco, son of Elizur Dudley, born Feb. 11, 1807, died Dec. 2, 1853.

Florilla Spencer.

585 *Blake*

Harvey B. Leete, son of George (281), m. 1st, Cynthia Clark. She died Oct. 10, 1871. He m. 2d, May 13, 1874, Mary E. Isbell, born Sept. 6, 1839.

955. Ollie A., b. July 27, 1850, d. in 1881. [1871.
956. George, Oct. 3, 1852, d. shot by accident,
957. Cynthia M., April 10, 1858.
958. Harvey B., Jr., June 16, 1859.
959. William P., Dec. 18, 1864.

960. George H., April 21, 1875.
961. Hattie L., Feb. 15, 1878.

597

Simeon A. Leete, son of Jared (292), m. Apr. 5, 1840, Adelia Blake, dau. of Reuben Blake and Chloe Adkins, of Middletown, born Nov. 12, 1803. She died June 29, 1876. He m. 2d, Sarah Miles, of Newtown, Conn., born Mar. 31, 1833. Residence, North Guilford.

962. Edwin Augustus, b. May 27, 1841, m. S. E. Dagle.
963. Charlotte Elizabeth, Feb. 24, 1843, m. H. C. Ball.
964. Juliet, April 26, 1845. m. W. R. Dean.
965. Lucy Ann, Mar. 19, 1847, m. J. C. Smith.

598 *Blake*

Clarissa Leete, dau. of Jared (292), m. Jan. 9, 1834, Roswell Blake, of Guilford, son of Reuben Blake and Chloe Adkins, of Middletown. He died, aged 73, June 24, 1873.

Jane Ann, b. Sept. 19, 1835, m. Edw. Kenney.
George M., Sept. 25, 1837, s. died in the war at Salisbury, N. C.
M. Luther, Dec. 9, 1839, m. E. M. Beers.
John R., May 10, 1848, d. Mar. 29, 1880.

599 *Blakeslee*

Lucina Leete, dau. of Jared (292), m. Julius Blakeslee, of Fair Haven.

Edward, died in the war.
Charles, of Aurora, Ill.

600   *Hotchkiss*

Parne Leete, dau. of Jared (292), m. John Hotchkiss, son of Joel. He died in 1852. She m. 2d, Philander Robinson.

Emogen,   m. Isaac Brown.
Charles.

601

Wm. H. Leete, son of Simeon (294), m. Oct. 15, 1848, Sylvia A. Kelsey, dau. of James Kelsey, of Madison, and Mary E. Camp, born July 21, 1830. She died, aged 21, Dec. 5, 1861. He m. 2d, Susan A. Tracy, dau. of John Tracy, of Colchester, and Lucy Warner, born May 12, 1842. He died Feb. 7, 1866.

     966. James Andrew, b. Nov. 4, 1849, d. Feb. 7, 1850.
     967. Katie Sylvia,   Jan. 15, 1860.
     968. Eva Annette,   Aug. 16, 1865, d. Feb. 20, 1866.

601½   *Dowd*

Elizabeth Leete, dau. of James A. (296), m. 1st, Henry Dowd, son of Rufus Dowd, of Madison. She m. 2d, Sept. 15, 1857, James W. Fowler, of North Guilford. No children.

602

James A. Leete, son of James A. (296), m. ―――― McCarthy. Went to California. Had two sons.

603   *Webster*

Ursula Leete, dau. of James A. (296), m. Daniel Webster. Resides in New York City.

604   *Nettleton*

Mary Ann Leete, dau. of James A. (296), m. May 7, 1854, Edwin Nettleton, of Killingworth, son of Bani Nettleton, born Nov., 1829. Removed to Clintonville in North Haven.

Sarah Eleanora, b. June 8, 1857, d. April 5, 1864.
Marion Sophronia, May 26, 1860, d. April 3, 1864.
James Edwin, Nov. 5, 1864.

605

Sophronia Leete, dau. of James A. (296), m. 1st, Oct. 19, 1851, Phineas L. Squire; 2d, Gilbert Page, of North Haven. No children.

606

John Wm. Leete, son of James A. (296), m. 1st, Julia ———; 2d, Adeline ———. He went to Meriden. All their children, five sons, aged 10 to 1, died of diphtheria in Jan., 1878.

607 *Camp*

Sarah A. Leete, dau. of James A. (296), m. Oct. 23, 1861, Sherman E. Camp, of Durham.

   Lillie.
   Carrie.
   James.

608 *Church*

Susan M. Leete, dau. of James A. (296), m. Mar. 7, 1867, Harrison H. Church. They have four children. Residence, Durham.

609

Orton R. Leete, son of James A. (296), m. 1st, Emma Stockwell, born in Milford, N. Y., Mar. 4, 1842. He m. 2d, June 17, 1877, Mary J. Clark. He went to San Francisco.

   969. Marian Roselle, b. Jan. 1, 1866, d. Sept. 17, 1866.
   970. James Franklin, Nov. 3, 1867.
   971. George Warren, Dec. 14, 1869.
   972. Ethel.

610

Elsie M. Leete, dau. of James A. (296), m. Merwin Palmer, of North Haven. He lost one arm in the war. They have had seven children, four of whom are now living.

614

William A. Leete, son of Alonzo (301), m. Dec. 25, 1869, Alice G. White, of Cheshire. They reside in Williamstown, Mass.

    973. Robert W., b. Dec. 28, 1871, d. Nov. 1, 1881, killed while playing between two cars.
    974. Howard A.,   Oct. 11, 1873.
    975. Arthur F.,   April 5, 1878.
    976. Leon G.,   April 11, 1883.

615

Oliver E. Leete, son of Alonzo (301), m. Jennie M. Parker. They have no children.

616

Marietta Leete, dau. of Alonzo (301), m. John B. Mowry.

    Ida L.,   May,   1879.
    Franklin J.,   May,   1881.
    George O.,   April 6, 1883.

617

Ida Leete, dau. of Alonzo (301), m. Albert Moon, of Pownall, Vt. She died May 29, 1883.

    Lester A.,   Aug. 7, 1881.
    Estella M.,   May 19, 1883.

619

Gilbert Luther Leete, son of Luther (302), m. Amelia Rathburn, of Williamstown, Mass.

977. Gilbert Nathaniel b.

620

George W. Leete, son of Luther (302), m. Cynthia Ashley, of Leverett, Mass.

621

William H. Leete, son of Luther (302), m. widow Mary Hawkes, of Leverett, Mass.

625 *Shipman*

Abbie Jane Leete, dau. of Samuel M. (304), m. in 1846, Edward E. Shipman. She died in 1849.

Achsah Adelia, b. Oct. 18, 1847.

626

Charles D. Leete, son of Samuel M. (304), m. Jan. 12, 1847, H. A. Richardson, born Feb. 12, 1825.

978. Charles S.,   b. Oct. 30, 1847, m. Martha Smith.
979. Herbert A., April 21, 1851, m. S. M. Williams.

627

Wm. A. Leete, son of Samuel M. (304), m. Aug. 29, 1854, Helen Spear.

980. Mary Jane,   b. June 11, 1858, m. J. C. Stoughton.
981. Francis Marion, Jan. 26, 1861.
982. Rosa L.,   Feb. 18, 1863, m. R. Thompson.
983. Anna Luella, Mar. 21, 1871.
984. George Keeler, Dec. 21, 1874.

629

John M. Leete, son of Samuel M. (304), m. Sept. 1, 1843, Sarah Tucker.

985. Horace F.,	b. June 29, 1864.	
986. Frederic,	Aug. 5, 1868.	
987. Annie A.,	Dec. 8, 1871, d. Dec. 18, 1874.	
988. Sarah L.,	Mar. 31, 1874, d. Dec. 29, 1874.	
989. Arthur A.,	Sept. 22, 1875.	
990. Mary H.,	Oct. 4, 1878.	

630   *Cole*

Rachel A. Leete, dau. of Samuel M. (304), m. Nov. 18, 1857, E. B. Cole.

Clinton Parker, b. Aug. 4, 1858, d. Feb. 18, 1859.
Flora Martha,   Oct. 29, 1859, m. C. L. Nickerson.
Jennie Mariet,   Aug. 29, 1861, m. D. R. Kershaw.
•Charles Edward,   Oct. 2, 1863.

631   *Higgins*

Mary E. Leete, dau. of Samuel M. (304), m. Mar. 4, 1861, Prentice Higgins.

Effie Maria,   b. Jan. 5, 1862, d. July 21, 1882.
Eddie M.,   Sept. 5, 1863, d. Sept. 6, 1865.
Wm. Sherman,   July 16, 1865.
Nellie May,   Aug. 17, 1867, d. Nov. 1, 1868.
Albert Grant,   Aug. 30, 1869.
Carrie Maude,   Mar. 6, 1872.
Frank Leonard,   Feb. 2, 1874.
Amy Mabel,   Feb. 6, 1876.
Anna Atwood,   April 15, 1878.
Nathan Prentice,   Dec. 11, 1880.
Mary Abbie,   Jan. 14, 1883.

634   *Emmons*

Harriet L. Leete, dau. of John C. (305), m. July 20, 1850, Asahel T. Emmons.

    Rachel Amelia, b. July 17, 1851, m. E. J. Watrous.
    Egbert G.,   Feb. 26, 1854, m. Eliza Clark.
    Hattie L.,   July 7, 1859.
    Allen A.,   Feb. 16, 1863.
    George C.,   Sept. 9, 1865.

635

Joseph H. Leete, son of John C. (305), m. Nov. 30, 1860, Maria Post.

    991. Evaline M.,   b. Mar. 13, 1862.
    992. Jennie O.,   April 3, 1863.
    993. Emma G.,   Mar. 26, 1867.
    994. Ida U.,   Aug. 8, 1869.
    995. Josephine E., Oct. 28, 1871.
    996. Joseph H.,   April 27, 1878.
    997. Charles U.,   Nov. 6, 1882.

636

Eliza C. Leete, dau. of John C. (305), m. Jan. 6, 1868, Edward F. Parker. No children.

637   *Alexander*

Sarah J. Leete, dau. of John C. (305), m. Dec. 6, 1865, John Alexander.

    Geo. Henry,   b. May 19, 1867.
    Eddie F.,   May 25, 1873.

639

Col. Geo. K. Leete, son of Edward A., Jr. (309), m. Feb. 18, 1864, Sarah B. Bryan. He enlisted into the army as a private in the Chicago Mercantile Battery. While serving in this capacity, he was detailed to act as clerk or secretary for Gen. Grant with the rank of Captain, and not long after was promoted to a place on Gen. Grant's staff with the rank of Colonel, which position he held till Gen. Grant resigned. He died, aged 44, Mar. 26, 1881.

998. Grant,   b. Mar. 23, 1866.
999. Mary,   Mar. 7, 1868.
1000. Alfred Bryan,   Dec. 17, 1869.
1001. George Keller,   July 22, 1872.
1002. Eliza Bryan,   July 23, 1881, posthumous.

642

Sarah E. Leete, dau. of Chauncey (344), m. William H. Edwards.

645   *Ford*

Mary Jane Leete, dau. of Geo. A. (311), m. Mar. 18, 1869, Chas. B. Ford.

Geo. Edwin,   b. May 29, 1871.
Wallace Elmer, May 22, 1873.

646

Geo. F. Leete, son of Geo. A. (311), m. Apr. 26, 1871, M. Hattie Remington. He resides in Providence, agent of several lines of steam-ships, etc.

647   *Foster*

Elizabeth J. Leete, dau. of Geo. A. (311), m. Apr. 23, 1874, Edward W. Foster, of Providence, R. I.

Geo. Edward,   b. April 30, 1879.
Ralph Leete,   May 20, 1881.
Charles Hosmer, Nov. 10, 1882.

648

Wm. A. Leete, son of Geo. A. (311), m. Nov. 25, 1879, Sophia E. Rawson.

1103. Millicent R., b. Aug. 28, 1880.
1004. Percy Remington, April 1, 1883.

654

Kitty M. Leete, dau. of Ira O. (313), m. Sachariah Adams.

660 *Powers*

Sarah Leete, dau. of Henry W. (324), m. John Powers. He went to Illinois and died there, leaving four or five children.

661

Henry E. Leete, son of Henry W. (324), m. Cynthia Freeman. He went to Geneva, Ashtabula Co., Ohio, where he died.

1005. William.
1006. George.
1007. Alice.

662

George Leete, son of Henry W. (324), m. Mary Coughlan. Residence, Thompsonville, Conn.

1008. Eva A.
1009. George.
1010. Arthur.
1011. William.
1012. Joseph.
1013. Edmund.
1014. daughter.

663 *Smith*

Elizabeth Leete, dau. of Henry W. (324), m. William Smith, who died in Hartford.

    Edmund,   of Windsor Locks.

664 *Conklin*

Marietta Leete, dau. of Henry W. (324), m. Alfred K. Conklin, of Brooklyn, N. Y. She died, aged 39, June 22, 1875.

    Mary Isabel,   b. Jan. 10, 1864.
    Irene Russell.

666 *Anderson*

Fanny A. Leete, dau. of Henry A. (324), m. John Anderson, of Windsor Locks.

    Albert.
    Mary.
    William.
    daughter.

667

Daniel S. Leete, son of Benjamin C. (325), m. Oct. 3, 1851, Cornelia I. Norton, dau. of Calvin Norton and Charlotte Morse, of Guilford, born Aug. 3, 1831. Residence, Guilford.

    1015. Henry Ives,   b. Jan. 16, 1854, d. April 20, 1855.
    1016. Nelson Sherwood, April 19, 1856, m. G. Benedict.
    1017. Fanny Amanda,   May 15, 1862, m. J. A. Coville.
    1018. Eva Rose.   Jan. 18, 1869.

668 *Lee*

Charity Leete, dau. of Benjamin C. (325), m. as second wife, April 3, 1853, Wm. H. Lee, of Guilford and New Haven. She died without children, aged 22, Aug. 2, 1854.

669

Justin O. Leete, son of Benjamin C. (325), m. May 25, 1856, Laura B., dan. of Geo. A. Kirkham and Julia Towner, of Guilford, born Feb. 17, 1836. She died, aged 27, Aug. 2, 1863. He died Mar. 5, 1863, aged 28.

1019. Henry B.,	b. Nov. 4, 1857, m Louisa Quist.	
1020. Infant son,	Nov. 4, 1857, d. Nov. 6, 1857.	
1021. Jennie Amanda,	Mar. 18, 1859.	

670 *Gauchet*

Sarah P. Leete, dau. of Benjamin C. (325), m. Jan. 6, 1853, Peter A. Gauchet, born near Paris, France, Jan. 9, 1819. Residence, Guilford.

Edward A.,	b. Aug. 23, 1854, m. M. A. Redding.
Mary,	June 29, 1856, d. June 29, 1856.
Lewis Leete,	July 23, 1857.
James Adolphus,	Oct. 27, 1860, m. Alga ———.
Daniel Benjamin,	Jan. 27, 1865.
Frank Henry,	Sept. 7, 1869.

671 *Ross*

Mary Jane Leete, dau. of Benjamin C. (325), m. Jan. 1, 1860, Geo. L. Ross, of Guilford, son of Noah W. Ross and Minerva Saxton, born Sept. 13, 1839. Residence, Guilford.

Geo. Edmund, b. Sept. 21, 1860, d. Dec. 10, 1860.

672

Douglas M. Leete, son of Benjamin C. (325), went to Texas. He married there and has one daughter.

1022.

673   *Pierson*

Emily C. Leete, dau. of Benjamin C. (325), m. Feb. 26, 1862, Heman Pierson, of Clinton. He died in the war Dec. 25, 1863. She died, aged 21, Nov. 25, 1864. Residence, Clinton, Conn.

    Orlestes Cook, b. Mar. 6, 1863, d. Jan. 18, 1876.

674   *Hurlbut*

Adeline A. Leete, dau. of Benjamin C. (325), m. Nov. 18, 1869, James Hurlbut, of Middletown, born in Wethersfield, June 16, 1845.

    Wm. Russell.
    Geo. Benjamin.
    Arthur Sherwood.
    Walter Leete,   Aug. 31, 1877.
    Albert Roland,   Aug. 7, 1880.
    Emma Maud,   July 24, 1882.

675

Judson W. Leete, son of Samuel W. (327), m. 1st, June 1, 1857, Rosetta Hill, dau. of Abraham G. Hill and Roxana Field, of Madison, born Nov. 11, 1838. She died without children, aged 19, Aug. 26, 1858. He m. 2d, Oct. 25, 1860, Helen L. Wilcox, dau. of Zina E. Wilcox and Lydia A. Hill, of Madison, born June 6, 1842. Residence, Leete's Island.

    1023. Charles Wyllis, b. April 20, 1861.
    1024. Adeline Jennette, May 25, 1863, d. Oct. 24, 1865.
    1025. Minnie Elizabeth, Dec. 2, 1864, d. Oct. 21, 1865.
    1026. Clarence Edwin, Aug. 31, 1870.
    1027. Josephine,   May 25, 1873.
    1028. Burdette S.,   Sept. 5, 1878.

676

Charles S. Leete, son of Sidney W. (330), m. Dec. 5, 1849, Olivia M. Cannon, dau. of LeGrand Cannon and Mary E. Trowbridge, of New Haven, born Aug. 21, 1828. He is a merchant in New Haven, dealing in drugs, chemicals, etc., and has been successful in business. He is also president of the Mechanics Bank of New Haven.

    1029. Ida Louisa,   b. Dec. 18, 1857.
    1030. Jeremiah Bishop, Dec. 29, 1862.

677   *Dickerman*

Mary Catharine Leete, dau. of Sidney W. (330), m. Wm. Dickerman, as third wife, March, 1864. She died, aged 39, Jan. 23, 1865.

678

Mary Ann Leete, dau. of Dea. Albert A. (331), m. as second wife, Jan. 1, 1855, Edwin A. Leete (701).

679

Sidney W. Leete, son of Dea. Albert A. (331), m. Oct. 24, 1862, Isabelle H. Clark, dau. of Dr. Atherton and Harriet S. Clark, of East Hampton, Mass., born Nov. 11, 1834. Residence, Guilford. Farmer.

682   *Parmelee*

Martha E. Leete, dau. of Dea. Albert A. (331), m. Jan. 18, 1869, Samuel S. Parmelee, son of Uriah N. Parmelee and Nancy Spencer, of Guilford, born Mar. 31, 1843. They removed to Augusta and to Macon, Ga.

    Laura Cornelia, b. April 3, 1870.
    Elizabeth Morris, Dec. 29, 1872.
    Catharine Ward, April 10, 1875.

684

Lewis B. Leete, son of Ambrose W. (333), m. Aug., 1883, Sarah E. Snow, dau. of David Snow and Mary Sisson, of East Haddam, Conn.

686

Edward Walter Leete, son of Dea. Edward L. (337), m. Oct. 10, 1861, Harriet Rogers, dau. of Daniel L. Rogers and Harriet Pratt, of Cornwall, Conn., born June 13, 1838. Farmer. Residence, Leete's Island.

1031. Abbie Louisa, b. Oct. 20, 1862.
1032. Edward Rogers, Dec. 17, 1864.
1033. Wm. Smith, Oct. 22, 1867.
1034. Sarah Talcott, Oct. 25, 1871.
1035. Walter, July 15, 1874, d. July 18, 1874.

687 *Rogers*

Lucy L. Leete, dau. of Dea. Edward L. (337), m. Dec. 16, 1863, Dwight Rogers, son of Daniel L. Rogers and Harriet Pratt, of Cornwall, born Aug. 3, 1832. Residence, Cornwall, Conn.

Dwight Leete, b. Dec. 11, 1866.
Nellie Lucretia, Nov. 12, 1868.
Harriet Fowler, Jan. 22, 1872.
Miner Pratt, Mar. 19, 1874.
Sylvia Abbie, Nov. 11, 1877.

[It is a tradition in this Rogers family, and it appears to be well founded, that they are lineal descendants of Rev. John Rogers the martyr, who, in 1555, by the orders of a popish queen, was burned at the stake in Smithfield, "in the presence," as the New England Primer has it, "of his wife and nine small children and one [of them] at the breast, at which sorrowful sight he was not in the least daunted, but died courageously for the gospel of Jesus Christ."] T.

688 *Bishop*

Nancy M. Leete, dau. of Rufus N. (338), m. as second wife, Feb. 12, 1862, Walter G. Bishop, of Meriden, born June 26, 1827. Residence, Guilford.

    Dexter Leete, b. Aug. 8, 1865.
    Burton Walter,) Jan. 25, 1867.
    Ellen Maria, (Jan. 25, 1867, d. Feb., 1867.
    Grace Sylvina, Sept. 10, 1873.

689

Richard M. Leete, son of Rufus N. (338), m. Nov. 14, 1861, Mary E. Norton, dau. of Anson Norton and Fanny Norton of Guilford, born Jan. 3, 1840. Residence, Leete's Island.

    1036. Anson Miner, b. Jan. 19, 1863.
    1037. Arthur Bishop, Jan. 13, 1864.
    1038. Ellsworth Norton. June 26, 1866.
    1039. Jennie Elizabeth, June 27, 1868.
    1040. Fanny Helen, Feb. 3, 1870.
    1041. Sarah Ellen, April 19, 1872.
    1042. Carrie May. Mar. 20, 1875, d. Mar. 29, 1875.

690

Roger C. Leete, son of Rufus N. (338), m. Oct., 1869, Helen A. Park, dau. of Amos Park and Arlette Griffing, of Sheshequin, Pa., born May 14, 1837. Residence, Leete's Island.

    1043. Irving P., b. Jan. 22, 1875.
    1044. Roger Wayne, Aug. 9, 1876.

694 *Chapman*

Ella Louisa Leete, dau. of Rev. Theodore A. (339), m. Aug. 24, 1875, Edward F. Chapman, of New Haven, now of Chicago.

Ethel, b. June 29, 1876.
Theodore Leete, Jan. 9, 1878.
Catharine Forrest, Jan. 3, 1880.
Edward Russell, July 28, 1881.

695

Rev. Wm. W. Leete, son of Rev. Theodore A. (339), m. April 4, 1883, Sarah E. Rockwell, dan. of Joel L. Rockwell and Ann Eliza Lounsbury, of Ridgefield, Conn., born Dec 14, 1857. He is a graduate of Amherst College, 1877, and of Yale Theological Seminary, and pastor of the Congregational Church in Ridgefield, Conn.

698

Abigail M. Leete, dan. of Alvan (342), m. Feb. 5, 1840, Ambrose W. Leete (333).

699 *Robbins*

Eliza Ann Leete, dan. of Alvan (342), m. May 23, 1850, Chauncey Robbins, of Wethersfield, born Jan. 28, 1808.

    John Leete, b. May 18, 1852. d. June 9, 1852.
    Chauncey Wood, Aug. 23, 1853.
    Elizabeth Palmer, May 26, 1856, d. Oct. 17, 1870.
    Edwin Leete, Aug. 12, 1858.
    Martha Mills, May 5, 1860.

700

Dr. Isaac P. Leete, son of Alvan (342), m. Mar. 16, 1843, Clarissa L. Foote, dan. of Jonathan Foote, of Branford, born June 12, 1821. He is a physician and formerly practiced in Branford, since in Suffield, Conn.

    1045. Lucy Gertrude, b. Mar. 18, 1848, m. Addison L. Abell.
    1046. Emma Evangeline, Sept. 6, 1852, m. Virgil M. Cooke.
    1047. Martha Clarissa, June 14, 1858, m. G. F. Reynolds.
    1048. Nellie Elizabeth, Mar. 3, 1861.

701

Dea. Edwin A. Leete, son of Alvan (342). m. 1st, Nov. 25, 1847, S. Ellen Hotchkiss, dau. of Eber S. Hotchkiss and Fanny Norton, of Guilford, born Nov. 10, 1825. She died, aged 28, July 3, 1854, leaving two children. He m. 2d, Jan. 1, 1855, Mary Ann Leete (678). Is a cabinet maker.

1049. Fanny Rebecca, b. Oct. 23, 1848, m. Ezra S. Kelsey.
1050. James Spencer, Sept. 8, 1850, d. Mar. 23, 1857.

1051. Edward Morris, Aug. 18, 1858, m. Eva Bishop.
1052. Catharine Ward, Nov. 28, 1860.
1053. Elizabeth Morris, Feb. 10, 1867.
1054. Wm. Henry, Dec. 3, 1868.

705

Lucy M. Leete, dau. of Morris A. (344). m. Feb. 7, 1866, Calvin M. Leete (340).

706

Geo. C. Leete, son of Morris A. (344). m. Sept. 22, 1850, Harriet L. Stebbins, dau. of Cyrus D. Stebbins and Nancy Beach, born in New Paltz, N. Y., June 9, 1827. Residence, Guilford.

1055. Geo. Henry, b. Dec. 17, 1851.
1056. Charles Edward, July 18, 1857, d. June 2, 1859.
1057. Frederic Darius, Nov. 17, 1859, d. June 7, 1865.
1058. Anna Mary, b. June 11, 1861.

707

Harvey W. Leete, son of Morris A. (344), m. July 4, 1855, Christiana P. Faulkner, dau. of Charles H. Faulkner and Ann Roberts, of Georgetown, S. C., born April 20, 1832. Residence, Guilford.

1059. Henry Walter, b. May 17, 1856, m. Hattie Prout.
1060. Robert Clyde, Sept. 14, 1859.

709

Joseph A. Leete, son of Morris A. (344), m. Jan. 15, 1859, Orphana K. Hill, dau. of Samuel B. Hill and Orphana Kelsey, of Madison, born May 8, 1840. Residence, Guilford.

1061. Elizabeth Hill, b. Dec. 17, 1860, m. Charles A. Hull.
1062. Clara Isabella,   July 9, 1864.

710   *Norton*

Lucinda J. Leete, dau. of Frederic W. (345), m. Sept. 13, 1847, John Norton, son of John B. Norton and Patty Brockett, of Guilford, born May 5, 1826. He died in the army, Dec. 25, 1862. She m. 2d, John Johnson, and died, aged 43, April 17, 1873.

    Charles Henry, b.   1849.
    Mary Elizabeth,   June 28, 1851, d. Jan. 26, 1853.
    Nellie,   Feb. 15, 1857, d. June 30, 1857.

    Bessie,   d.

711   *Norton*

Amelia C. Leete, dau. of Frederic W. (345), m. Sept. 18, 1850, Henry W. Norton, son of John B. Norton and Patty Brockett, of Guilford, born July 31, 1818. Residence, Leete's Island.

    Ellen Amelia,   b. April 12, 1851, d. Sept. 23, 1851.
    Alice Adelia,   Feb. 18, 1854, m. Frederic Butler.
    Lucy Amelia,   Feb. 6, 1855, m. Geo. Watrous.
    Wm. Henry,   Dec.,   1857.

712

Gilbert W. Leete, son of Frederic W. (345), m. Mar. 12, 1860, Esther Maria Scoville, of Middletown, born in Collinsville, Aug. 8, 1840. They reside in Leete's Island, having no children.

713

Nelson F. Leete, son of Frederic W. (345), m. April 29, 1863, Maria A. Dunn, dau. of John Dunn and Juliet Bradley, of Guilford, born April 14, 1838. Residence, Guilford. He died Dec. 16, 1883, aged 44.

1063. Frederic, b. Feb. 9, 1867.

715

Joel F. Leete, son of Frederic W. (345), m. Jan. 25, 1875, Clara M. Norton, dau. of Joseph Norton and Susan O. Morgan, of Guilford, born May 25, 1854.

1064. Murray B., b. May 29, 1878.

716

Allen N. Leete, son of Allen N. (346), m. Emma Luckey.

1065. Edward.

717

Charles W. Leete, son of Rev. Charles W. (348), m. in 1850, Eliza Willes, born in 1827. They are of Potsdam, N. Y.

1066. Harriet A., b. Jan. 31, 1852. [Y. C. 1879.
1067. Charles Henry, Mar. 17, 1857, m. Isadore A. Kelton,
1068. Edward Willes, Jan. 13, 1859.

718

Allen N. Leete. son of Rev. Charles W. (348), m. Abigail Button. He removed to Clarksville, Iowa.

1069. Charles.
1070. Jennie.

720

Wilbur F. Leete, son of Rev. Charles W. (348), m. Nov. 7, 1867, Antoinette Church, born Oct. 24, 1845. They reside in Oneida, N. Y.

1071. Wm. Church, b. June 3, 1870.
1072. Wilford Arthur, April 27, 1872.

721

Sophronia Leete, dau. of Rev. Charles W. (348), m. E. G. Church.

722

Wm. S. Leete, son of Rev. Charles W. (348), m. in 1866, Rose A. Fleming, born in 1845. They reside in Oneida, N. Y.

1073. Adaline Rosella, b.   1878.

724

Robert B. Leete, son of Harley N. (349), m. Dec. 22, 1852, S. E. Cummings. He is a merchant of Verona, N. Y.

1074. Jessie,   b. Feb. 9, 1857, m. Dr. —— Lewis.
1075. Harley,   Dec. 1, 1863.
1076. Carrie,   July 12, 1866.

725

Sarah E. Leete, dau. of Harley N. (349), m. Delos W. Gibbs.

728   *Barnhart*

Mary J. Leete, dau. of Simeon (359), m. Hiram Barnhart.

    Harriet.
    Franklin.

729

Henry C. Leete, son of Simeon (359), m. Cordelia Gifford.

1077. Mary.
1078. Jennie.

730

Alfred D. Leete, son of Simeon (359), m. Ellen J. Strong, born Sept. 12, 1830.

1079. Helen,   b.   1865.
1080. Laura.

731 *Russell*

Helen Leete, dau. of Simeon (359), m. Thomas Russell.

Ida.

732 *Furlow*

Ann E. Leete, dau. of Simeon (359), m. Eber Furlow.

Martin.

733

Geo. L. Leete, son of Simeon (359), m. Georgiana ——.

1081. Hattie.

734 *Hull*

Martha Leete, dau. of Timothy (360), m. Andrew J. Hull.

    Cassius.
    Martha.
    Timothy.

736 *Ellsworth*

Mary Leete, dau. of Lewis (361), m. J. Ellsworth.

    Mary L.

737   *Strong*

Elizabeth Leete, dau. of Lewis (361), m. Gilbert Strong.

    Lewis.
    William.
    Nettie.
    Carlton.
    Robert.
    Arthur.

738   *Mye*

Ophelia Leete, dau. of Lewis (361), m. Harvey Mye.

    Carrie.
    Charlie.
    Mamie.

739   *Young*

Sarah Leete, dau. of Franklin (365), m. Charles Young.

740   *Geddes*

Caroline Leete, dau. of Franklin (365), m. D. H. Geddes.

741

Fayette G. Leete, son of Franklin (365), m. Helen Olds. Residence, Dewittville, N. Y.

    1082. Martha.
    1083. Franklin.

742

Charles S. Leete, son of Franklin (365), m. Lillie Haskins.

749

Anson G. Leete, son of Wm. (366), m. Annette Thompson, and lives in Washington, Iowa.

    1084. Lucy.
    1085. Willard.

751 and 752

Willis D. Leete and Geo. E. Leete, sons of Wm. (366), are merchants at Mayville and Chautauqua Point, N. Y.

757

Charles A. Leete, son of Alfred N. (374), m. Dec., 1879, Elizabeth Moorhead, born in 1854.

1086. Florence M., b. 1881.

760 *Moorhead*

Clara M. Leete, dau. of Calvin (375), m. in 1867, J. C. Moorhead, Assistant Superintendent Canada Southern Railroad. Residence, St. Thomas, Ont.

    Grace Eleanor, b. 1871.
    Clara Louise, 1873, d. 1874.
    Maud Eliza, 1875.

761 *Wagner*

Georgiana E. Leete, dau. of Calvin (375), m. Dec., 1875, T. S. Wagner, of Maple Hill, Waubonsaa Co., Kansas Farmer.

    Eleanor May, b. 1877.

766

Sherman M. Leete, son of Wm. P. (385), m. Nov. 15, 1868, Chloe Sherwin, dau. of Rev. John C. Sherwin. He died Aug. 1, 1878.

1087. Robert Guy, b. Feb. 1, 1871.
1088. Mary Ella, Jan. 17, 1876.

767

Joseph G. Leete, son of Wm. P. (385), m. Sept. 20, 1869, Ellen J. Pitkin, dau. of James Pitkin, of West Salem, Wis.

1089. Lucy Louisa, b. July 1, 1870.
1090. Darwin James, June 1, 1872.
1091. Herbert Nelson, July 5, 1874.
1092. Dwight Goodrich, Nov. 14, 1880.

768

Geo. H. Leete, son of Wm. P. (385), m. Oct. 1, 1872, Sarah Callahan, dau. of Hugh Callahan, of La Crosse, Wis.

1093. George, b. Oct. 22, 1874, d. July 1, 1875.
1094. Lizzie Hastings, June 17, 1876.

770

Wm. W. Leete, son of Wm. P. (385), m. Sept. 28, 1880, Kate Collins, of Winnebago. They reside at Moose Lake, Minn.

1095. Ruth, b. Dec. 21, 1881.
1096. Zaida, July 2, 1883.

771 *White*

Zaida L. Leete, dau. of Wm. P. (385), m. May 25, 1881, Charles Henry White. Residence, Marshall, Minn.

772

Frank E. Leete, son of Wm. P. (385), m. Dec. 31, 1883, Zaida Elizabeth Moran, dau. of Joseph Moran, of West Salem, Wis. She died, April 9, 1884, aged 19 years.

776

Louisa Arlena Leete, dau. of Col. Charles E. (393), is a missionary at Tokio, Japan.

777

Sarah A. Leete, dau. of Wm. J. (394), m. Dec. 23, 1875, John W. Ethridge.

    Lena, b. Oct. 27, 1876.
    William Harvey, Aug. 18, 1878.
    Annie Kate, Mar. 18, 1882.

789

Eugene F. Leete, son of James (417), of Claremont, N. H., m. June 21, 1868, Georgia Haynes. They reside in Boston, Mass.

790

Clarence M. Leete, son of James (417), of Claremont, N. H., m. Apr. 19, 1876, Minnie Ladd.

1097. Burtena A., b. Nov. 30, 1877.
1098. Jeffries W., April, 1882.

791

Wallace M. Leete, son of James (417), of Claremont N. H., m. Apr. 7, 1876, Madora A. Byron.

822

Seth P. Leete, son of Geo. W. (434), m. Dec. 24, 1874, Catharine Colwell, dau. of Rev. G. T. Colwell. He is a lawyer of Montreal.

1099. Eva Lucina, Oct. 21, 1876.
1100. Mabel Elizabeth, Aug. 21, 1878, d. March 4, 1879.
1101. Ernest Colwell, May 19, 1881.
1102. dau. April 10, 1883.

823 *Miner*

Orpha A. Leete, dau. of Geo. W. (434), m. Oct. 12, 1874, Wm. W. Miner, and resides in Granby, P. Q., Canada. He is a carriage maker.

    Sarah W., b. Aug. 6, 1875.
    Mary Lucina, April 7, 1877.
    Wm. Harlow, Dec. 16, 1879.

824

Warren R. Leete, son of Geo. W. (434), m. Mar. 18, 1877, Sarah Olney. They reside in Danville, P. Q., Canada. He is a photographer.

    1103. Etta Louisa, b. May 18, 1878.
    1104. James Garfield, Oct. 4, 1880.

826

Eddy M. Leete, son of Geo. W. (434), m. Sept. 11, 1883, Sadie Burbank. They reside in Lowell, Mass.

847

878

Sarah E. Leete, dau. of Chauncey (460), m. Wm. H. Edwards. Erroneously entered on page 124.

879 *Stephens*

Clarinda Leete, dau. of Dr. Albert E. (467), m. Sept. 19, 1853, Henry Stephens, of Detroit, Mich.

888 *Fitch*

Mary E. Leete, dau. of Asahel (472), m. T. H. Fitch.

896   *Wilson*

Harriet R. Leete, dau. of John (489), m. Apr. 29, 1874, Edward Wilson.

901   *Lane*

Sarah A. Leete, dau. of Josiah F. (525), m. Feb. 28, 1874, Jacob Lane, of Wallingford. He died in 1875 and she m. 2d, William Downs, of Madison.

903   *Perkins*

Eugenia H. Leete, dau. of Josiah F. (525), m. Oct. 16, 1882, Albert E. Perkins, of Chester. One child, born August, 1883.

910   *Penny*

Mary E. Leete, dau. of Thaddeus M. (527), m. Nov. 24, 1875, Robert L. Penny, of New Haven, a lawyer, removed to Minneapolis.

918

Harriet S. Leete, dau. of Geo. W. (532), m. Washington Jacobs. Residence, San Francisco. They have a dau. Maud, born 1866, and had a son who died in infancy.

919

Christine I. Leete, dau. of Geo. W. (532), m. Thomas Collins, of San Francisco.

    Robert Hilliard,   1879.
    Thomas Buell,   1882.
    Charles Henry,   1884.

921 *Woodhull*

Mattie J. Leete, dau. of Anson L. (524), m. May 29, 1867, Charles S. Woodhull, of Huntington, N. Y., born Aug. 21, 1844. He died June 28, 1875.

    Edith Anna,   b. Nov. 16, 1868.
    Eleanor Mabel,   Sept. 23, 1873.

931 *Hamilton*

Edith I. Leete, dau. of Ralph (543), m. John Hamilton.

935 *Strathers*

Elizabeth H. Leete, dau. of Lewis (557), m. John H. Strathers.

    Helen,   b. Feb. 28, 1849.
    William,   Oct. 14, 1855.
    Mary L.,   June 18, 1857.
    Agnes,   Jan. 17, 1860.

937 *Otto*

Mary C. Leete, dau. of Lewis (557), m. Charles W. Otto, of Philadelphia.

    Lizzie L.,   b. Sept. 30, 1859.

939 *Bradley*

Sarah A. Leete, dau. of Horace (558), m. Apr. 9, 1854, Charles Wm. Bradley, of East Haven.

940 *Eldridge*

Harriet E. Leete, dau. of Horace (558), m. Sept. 11, 1859, Eleazar L. Eldridge, of Sag Harbor, L. I.

942

John R. Leete, son of John R. (559), m. Susan T. Rowe, of Fair Haven.

946 *Smith*

Josephine C. Leete, dau. of Joshua G. (567) m. Sept. 30, 1868, Edward D. Smith, of Fair Haven. They removed to St. Peter's, Minn. Since returned to Fair Haven. He is in Second National Bank, New Haven.

    Mary Bell,   b. Sept. 23, 1871, d. July 7, 1871.
    James Edward,   Nov. 12, 1872.
    Effie Josephine,   Sept. 20, 1877.

948

Frank G. Leete, son of Joshua G. (567), m. May, 1880, Rachel A. Slawson.

1105. Mary Josephine, b. May,   1881.
1106. Frank Edgar,   Mar. 15, 1884.

949

Edgar C. Leete, son of Joshua G. (567), m. Dec., 1877, Mary E. Crane.

1107. David Joshua, b. Sept. 13, 1878.

962

Edwin A. Leete, son of Simeon A. (597), m. Feb. 11, 1863, Susan E. Dagle, of Wallingford, Conn., dau. of Daniel Reed, born Mar. 13, 1844. They reside in North Guilford and have no children.

963

Charlotte E. Leete, dau. of Simeon A. (597), m. Henry O. Ball, of North Branford, born Sept. 22, 1846. She died in North Guilford, Feb. 20, 1877.

    Geo. Henry,   b. Jan. 27, 1869.
    Phebe,   Dec. 3, 1870.

964   *Dean*

Juliet Leete, dau. of Simeon A. (597), m. Dec., 1864, Wm. R. Dean, of Meriden. He died in 1880.

    Minnie,   b.   about 1869.
    daughter,   d. aged 5.

965   *Smith*

Lucy A. Leete, dau. of Simeon A. (597), m. July 4, 1866, Joel C. Smith, son of Samuel Smith, of North Madison, born Feb. 18, 1848.

    Emma Sophia, b. Aug. 21, 1867, d. June 22, 1868.
    Perley Seymour, Oct. 22, 1868.
    Nellie Irene, Feb. 12, 1871, d. April 28, 1873.
    Herbert Franklin, Dec. 2, 1873.
    Frederic Lewis, July 6, 1875.
    Infant son, June 19, 1877, d. June 21, 1877.
    Alice Irene, July 12, 1878.

978

Charles S. Leete, son of Charles D. (626), m. Nov. 13, 1873, Martha Smith.

    1108. Albert D., b. July 26, 1875.
    1109. Alice,   Nov. 17, 1877.
    1110. Gracie A., May 2, 1880.

979

Herbert A. Leete, son of Charles D. (626), m. May 1, 1872, Sarah M. Williams. He died June 23, 1874. She died June 24, 1879.

1111. Mabel A., b. Feb. 4, 1873.

980 *Stoughton*

Mary J. Leete, dau. of Wm. A. (627), m. Sept. 1, 1881, J. C. Stoughton.

982 *Thompson*

Rosa L. Leete, dau. of Wm. A. (627), m. Dec. 29, 1881, Robert Thompson.

1016

Nelson S. Leete, son of Daniel S. (667), m. Apr. 23, 1878, Gertrude E. R. Benedict, of New Haven, born in Woodbridge, Sept. 25, 1857. They reside in Guilford.

1017 *Coville*

Fanny A. Leete, dau. of Daniel S. (667), m. Aug. 7, 1879, James A. Coville, born in Worcester, Mass. She died, aged 21, May 6, 1883.

    Minnie Ives, b. April 26, 1880.
    Alice Belle, Dec. 27, 1881, d. May 3, 1883.

1019

Henry B. Leete, son of Justin O. (669), m. Nov. 4, 1878, Louisa Quist, born in Gottenberg, Sweden, Oct. 12, 1859. Residence, Guilford.

    William Thomas, b. Feb. 9, 1884.

1045   *Abell*

L. Gertrude Leete, dau. of Dr. Isaac P. (700), m. Dec. 3, 1872, Addison L. Abell, born Dec. 27, 1844.

   G. Ethleen,   b. Mar. 28, 1880.

1046   *Cooke*

Emma E. Leete, dau. of Dr. Isaac P. (700), m. Apr. 25, 1874, Virgil M. Cooke, born July 19, 1845.

   Florence F.,   b. Nov. 22, 1877, d. July 30, 1878.
   Virginia,   June 21, 1879, d. April 23, 1880.
   E. Maude,   June 28, 1881

1047   *Reynolds*

Clarissa M. Leete, dau. of Dr. Isaac P. (700), m. June 17, 1880, Geo. Francis Reynolds.

   Grace Louisa Leete, b. July 25, 1882.

1049   *Kelsey*

Fanny Rebecca Leete, dau. of Dea. Edwin A. (701), m. Oct. 5, 1875, Ezra S. Kelsey, of Madison.

1051

Edward M. Leete, son of Dea. Edwin A. (701), m. Oct. 15, 1879, Eva S. Bishop, dau. of E. Chapman Bishop and Charlotte G. Fowler, of Guilford, born Apr. 19, 1859. Residence, Guilford.

   1112. Frank Chapman, b. Aug. 16, 1881.

1059

Henry W. Leete, son of Harvey W. (707), m. Hattie Prout, of Branford.

1061 *Hull*

Elizabeth H. Leete, dau. of Joseph A. (709), m. June 22, 1881, Charles E. Hull, son of Geo. A. Hull, and H. Jennette Bishop, of Guilford, born March 25, 1860.

Twin sons.   b. July 17, 1882, died soon.

1067

Charles H. Leete, son of Charles W. (717), m. 1883, Isadore A. Kelton, born 1860.

1074 *Lewis*

Jessie Leete, dau. of Robert B. (724), m. Dr. —— Lewis.

INDEX I.

NAMES OF LEETES.

Born.		Page.	Born.		Page.
1862	Abbie L.	130	1809	Almira,	56
	Abby C. (Royce),	50	1800	Almon,	35
1820	Abby J. (Shipman),	72	1829	Almon H.	59
1707	Abigail,	13	1817	Alonzo,	40
1683	Abigail (Bradley).	10	1822	Alonzo,	62
1762	Abigail (Chittenden).	24	1801	Alvah.	33
1830	Abigail (Kenerson),	54	1791	Alvan,	44
—	Abigail (Woodbridge).	9	1783	Amanda (Hand),	31
1816	Abigail M. (Leete),	80	1816	Amanda (McCord),	46
1814	Abigail W (Weld),	65	1807	Amanda J. (Pratt),	44
1753	Abner,	23	1808	Amanda M. (Day),	28
1779	Abner,	35	1753	Amasa,	23
1817	Abner B.	64	1770	Amasa,	36
1755	Abraham,	23	1748	Ambrose,	19
1784	Abraham,	30	1774	Ambrose,	30
	Abraham,	33	1809	Ambrose W.	43
1747	Absalom,	23	1831	Amelia C. (Norton),	81
1782	Absalom,	36	1758	Amos.	20
	Adah,	112	1769	Amos,	25
1757	Adam Raynor,	21	1790	Amos,	31
1794	Adam Raynor,	33	1833	Amos H.	47
1830	Adam R.	53	1775	Amy,	34
1832	Adam R.	53	1643	Andrew,	9
1844	Adelaide,	91	1713	Andrew,	16
1850	Adeline A. (Hurlbut),	75		Andrew,	25
1836	Adeline,	81		Andrew,	32
1863	Adeline J.	128	1700	Ann (Hopson),	15
1878	Adeline R.	136	1695	Ann (Smith),	17
1805	Albert A.	43	1756	Ann,	24
1820	Albert D.	64		Ann E. (Furlow)	83
1875	Albert D.	146	1830	Ann M.	76
1802	Albert E., Dr.	56	1726	Ann (Collins),	10
1797	Alexander,	39	1824	Ann (Elliott),	46
1861	Alexander D.	73	1726	Anna,	17
1869	Alfred B.	124	1757	Anna,	27
	Alfred D.	83	1728	Anna,	16
1818	Alfred N.	46	1826	Anna (Hall),	47
	Alice,	125	1791	Anna (Leete),	38
1877	Alice,	146		Anna (Tracy),	38
1878	Alice I.	146	1661	Anna (Trowbridge),	9
	Alice M	98	1859	Anna E.	111
1728	Allen,	18	1871	Anna L.	121
1840	Allen B.	73	1861	Anna M.	133
1793	Allen N.	44	1871	Annie A.	122
1825	Allen N.	81	1779	Augustus,	30
1839	Allen N.	81	1871	Barbara E.	110
	Almeda (Brooks),	33		Bates,	31
	Alpha,	41	1828	Belinda (Barnum),	52
1802	Alpha C. (Orcutt),	28	1686	Benjamin,	10

Born.		Page.	Born.		Page.
1717	Benjamin,	14	1861	Charles W.	128
1753	Benjamin,	21	1843	Charlotte E. (Ball),	117
	Benjamin,	32	1843	Charlotte U.	81
1809	Benjamin,	49	1806	Chauncey,	55
1804	Benjamin C.	42		Chauncey W.	101
1831	Benjamin F.	58	1854	Cherilla E.	109
	B. Franklin.	64	1730	Chloe (Ranney),	17
1875	Bertha,	110	1791	Chloe (Vesey),	33
1793	Betsey (Moore),	38	1855	Chloe,	72
1800	Betsey (King),	55	1839	Chloe A. (Hall),	53
1798	Betsey B. (Leete),	44	1849	Christinna I. (Collins),	110
1816	Betsey E. (Chapman),	63	1832	Clara.	66
1868	Betsey J.	109	1876	Clara,	107
1878	Burdette,	128	1864	Clara I.	134
1877	Burlena A.	141	1870	Clarence E.	128
1867	Burton W.	131	1850	Clarence M.	93
1651	Caleb.	9	1834	Clarence P.	103
1673	Caleb,	10	1804	Clarinda (Burton),	56
1708	Caleb.	15	1814	Clarinda (Beebe),	55
1819	Calvin,	46	1832	Clarinda (Stephens).	103
1759	Calvin.	26	1832	Clarinda H.	59
1822	Calvin D.	58	1789	Clarissa (Stone).	38
1851	Calvin E.	88		Clarissa,	41
1816	Calvin M.	43	1818	Clarissa (Hepburn),	48
1867	Calvin M.	79	1823	Clarissa (Willey),	52
1810	Caroline (Vorce),	45	1815	Clarissa (Blake),	69
	Caroline (Lippit),	58	1845	Clarissa M. (Moorhead),	88
	Caroline (Geddes),	85	1865	Cora A.	99
1820	Caroline A. (Walkley),	46	1867	Cora G.	93
1866	Carrie,	136	1862	Cora I.	87
1855	Carrie E.	109	1860	Cora A.	87
1846	Catharine A. (Parker),	77	1842	Cordelia E.	72
1811	Catharine W.	43		Clinton,	100
1860	Catharine W.	133		Cynthia (Wynne),	27
1863	Celia O.	98	1819	Cynthia E. (Wilcox),	40
1832	Charity (Lee),	75	1858	Cynthia M.	117
	Charles,	49	1802	Cyrus.	33
	Charles,	50	1836	Cyrus,	53
	Charles,	135		Cyrus A.	48
1853	Charles A.	87	1709	Daniel,	13
1856	Charles B.	73	1721	Daniel,	14
1860	Charles B.	74	1742	Daniel,	19
1849	Charles D.	77	1773	Daniel,	29
1826	Charles E.	48		Daniel,	32
1857	Charles E.	99		Daniel,	49
1857	Charles E.	133	1781	Daniel Brown,	38
1820	Charles F.	43	1816	Daniel M.	65
1857	Charles F.	93		Darwin,	94
1857	Charles H.	135	1872	Darwin J.	140
1823	Charles L.	40		David,	31
1868	Charles M.	98	1821	David E.	63
1823	Charles S.	76	1878	David I.	145
	Charles S.	85	1800	David M.	33
1823	Charles S.	72	1839	Delia P.	58
1847	Charles S.	121	1809	Dexter.	51
1882	Charles U.	123	1850	Dexter,	95
1799	Charles W.	44	1680	Dorothy (Hopson),	10
	Charles W.	81	1712	Dorothy (Hurd),	15
1864	Charles W.	89		Duron.	94
1865	Charles W.	91	1880	Dwight G.	140

Born	Name	Page	Born	Name	Page
1752	Eber,	20	1801	Emily A.	40
1780	Eber,	34		Emily (Griffing),	39
1860	Eddy M.	96	1843	Emily C. (Pierson),	75
1811	Edgar J.	56		Emma,	116
	Edith,	100	1852	Emma E. (Cooke),	132
1881	Edith G.	98	1867	Emma G.	123
1853	Edith I. (Hamilton),	112	1852	Emma L.	109
1872	Edith M.	93	1881	Ernest C.	141
1775	Edmund,	29	1798	Epaphras Nott.	35
	Edmund,	125	1824	Esther J. (Simmons),	58
1819	Edna (Salls),	55	1878	Etta L.	142
	Edwin,	50		Eunice (Wilson),	49
1822	Edwin A.	80	1807	Eunice C. (Young),	40
1841	Edwin A.	117	1817	Eunice L. (Field),	42
	Edwin,	64	1876	Eva L.	141
	Edward,	135		Eveline E. (Hinman),	63
1761	Edward A.	27	1724	Ezekiel,	14
1805	Edward A.	40	1751	Ezekiel,	21
1810	Edward L.	43		Ezra,	51
1858	Edward M.	133	1842	Fanny A. (Anderson),	75
1864	Edward R.	130	1862	Fanny A. (Coville),	126
1834	Edward Walter,	78	1860	Fanny F. (Seymour),	93
1859	Edward W.	135	1806	Fanny M. (Fowler),	42
1836	Eleanor (Denison),	53	1848	Fanny R. (Kelsey),	133
1785	Eli,	31		Fayette G.	85
1795	Eli,	34		Flora (Tanner),	39
1807	Eliza (Herrick),	45	1854	Flora (Heath),	91
	Eliza,	59	1881	Florence,	139
1803	Eliza A. (Haswell),	40	1861	Francis M.	121
1866	Eliza A.	85	1846	Frank,	86
1818	Eliza A. (Robbins),	80		Frank,	100
1881	Eliza B.	124	1881	Frank C.	148
1802	Eliza (Rice),	62	1858	Frank E.	89
1815	Eliza E. (Dudley),	67	1884	Frank E.	145
1702	Elizabeth,	15	1853	Frank H.	91
1750	Elizabeth (Smith),	23	1815	Franklin,	45
1787	Elizabeth (Snell),	33		Franklin,	138
1811	Elizabeth (Fitzgerald),	35	1841	Franklin M.	104
1785	Elizabeth (Stevens).	39		Fred,	100
1816	Elizabeth (Minor),	46	1875	Freddie R.	105
1838	Elizabeth (Bowen),	66		Frederic, Dr.	36
1820	Elizabeth (Dowd),	71	1860	Frederic,	112
1833	Elizabeth (Smith),	75	1868	Frederic,	122
	Elizabeth,	60	1867	Frederic,	135
	Elizabeth (Strong),	84	1859	Frederic D.	133
1859	Elizabeth S.	88	1865	Frederic K.	109
1824	Elizabeth H. (Strathers).	113	1803	Frederic W.	44
1845	Elizabeth C.	45	1836	Freeman,	54
1860	Elizabeth H. (Hull),	134		Gains,	33
1867	Elizabeth M.	133	1782	George,	38
1851	Elizabeth J. (Foster),	73		George,	39
1857	Ella E. (Holton),	95		George,	58
1853	Ella L. Chapman,	79	1830	George,	74
1826	Ellen A.	113		George,	94
	Ellen,	50	1852	George,	117
1840	Ellen L.	79		George,	125
	Elsie E.	85	1817	George A.	40
1848	Elsie M. (Palmer),	71	1834	George A.	66
1807	Emeline W. (Caldwell),	45	1820	George B.	65
1851	Emeline S.	77	1829	George C.	80

Born.		Page.	Born.		Page.
1862	George E.	85	1832	Hattie,	137
1875	George E.	93		Hattie,	100
1866	George E.	105		Hattie L.	85
1849	George F.	73		Helen (Russell),	83
1821	George H.	59	1865	Helen,	137
1849	George H.	89	1817	Henrietta,	62
1875	George H.	117	1805	Henry,	35
1851	George H.	133		Henry,	36
1858	George I.	99		Henry,	48
1836	George K.	73	1840	Henry,	53
1874	George K.	121	1847	Henry,	60
1872	George K.	124	1827	Henry A.	59
	George L.	83	1857	Henry B.	127
1847	George M.	110		Henry C.	83
1876	George O.	98	1828	Henry E.	74
	George W.	49	1801	Henry W.	42
1819	George W.	52	1832	Henry W.	80
1819	George W.	63	1856	Henry W.	133
1850	George W.	72	1873	Herbert D.	105
1851	George W.	91	1874	Herbert N.	140
1869	George W.	119	1847	Hiram,	54
1849	Georgiana E. (Wagner),	88		Homer,	39
1874	Gertie P.	98	1803	Horace,	55
1703	Gideon,	12		Horace,	31
1731	Gideon,	18	1810	Horace,	62
1765	Gideon.	27	1818	Horace,	63
1848	Gilbert L.	72		Horace,	64
1835	Gilbert M.	58	1861	Horace A.	109
	Gilbert N.	121	1864	Horace F.	122
1880	Gracie A.	146	1873	Howard A.	120
1866	Grant,	124	1858	Ida (Moon),	71
1848	Hallet,	103	1872	Ida B.	98
1739	Hannah,	17	1857	Ida L.	129
1749	Hannah (Howd),	23	1869	Ida U.	123
1813	Hannah,	40		Ira,	31
1808	Hannah (Fowler),	43	1821	Ira O.	40
1835	Hannah,	103	1875	Irving P.	131
1827	Hannah W. (Benton),	47	1864	Irwin J.	109
	Harley E.	41	1821	Isaac P.	80
	Harley N.	44	1830	Isabella A.	48
1864	Harley,	97	1833	Isabella E. (Hull),	65
	Harriet,	64		James,	64
	Harriet L.	59	1841	James,	95
1816	Harriet M.	63	1825	James A.	71
1816	Harriet S. (Fenner),	57	1838	James E.	103
1837	Harriet W. (Sullivan),	58	1867	James F.	119
1848	Harriet C.	77	1856	James P.	91
1840	Harriet E. (Eldridge),	113	1850	James S.	133
1828	Harriet G.	103	1882	Jeffries W.	141
1858	Harriet G.	109		Jennie,	135
	Harriet L. (Emmons),	72		Jennie,	137
1844	Harriet P.	103	1849	Jennie (Roy).	91
1846	Harriet R. (Wilson),	106	1859	Jennie A.	127
1844	Harriet S. (Jacobs),	110	1859	Jennie M.	105
1797	Harvey,	31	1863	Jennie C.	123
1793	Harvey,	34	1862	Jerome B.	129
1817	Harvey B.	67	1857	Jessie (Lewis),	136
1859	Harvey B.	117	1845	Joel F.	81
1798	Harvey H.	35	1821	Joel M.	80
1832	Harvey W.	80		John,	31

Born.		Page.	Born.		Page.
1853	John,	86	1851	Lizzie M. (Benedict),	77
1857	John A.	74		Lizzie M.	85
1842	John B.	73	1778	Lois (Bunnell),	34
1869	John H.	91	1792	Lois (Gould),	35
1834	John M.	72	1830	Loren,	53
	John R.	64		Lorenzo,	41
1834	John R.	113		Louisa,	49
	John T.	105	1874	Louisa,	107
1833	John W.	71	1855	Louisa A.	91
1859	Joseph,	72	1822	Louisa M.	43
	Joseph,	125	1781	Lovicia,	36
1836	Joseph A.	80	1817	Lucina (Blakeslee),	69
1847	Joseph G.	89	1743	Lucy (Barker),	16
1880	Joseph G.	142	1863	Lucy,	25
1833	Joseph H.	72	1763	Lucy,	27
1878	Joseph H.	123	1794	Lucy (Wilcox),	36
1848	Joseph F.	71		Lucy,	41
1873	Josephine,	128		Lucy (Loper),	55
1871	Josephine F.	123		Lucy (Winters),	60
1823	Jonathan F.	66		Lucy,	138
1824	Joshua G.	65	1806	Lucy A.	28
1866	J. Neely,	88	1847	Lucy A. (Smith),	117
1836	Judson W.	76	1848	Lucy G. (Abell),	132
	Julia,	64	1814	Lucy A. (Hull),	63
	Julia,	83	1839	Lucy L. (Rogers),	78
1822	Juliana (Newhall),	66	1870	Lucy L.	140
1845	Juliet A. (Dean),	117	1827	Lucy M. (Leete),	80
1834	Justin O.	75		Lucia (Cassidy),	33
1860	Katie S.	118		Lucinda (Thomas),	32
1862	Kenneth,	97	1829	Lucinda J. (Norton),	81
1849	Kitty M. (Adams),	74		Lucius,	41
1841	Laura (Clark),	69		Lucretia,	25
	Laura,	137	1820	Lucretia (Fenner),	57
1810	Laura A.	44	1812	Lucretia (Peck),	67
1844	Laura A. (Niles),	71	1776	Luranda,	25
1839	Laura C.	58	1819	Luther,	40
1865	Laura L.	95	1749	Lydia (Leete),	20
1853	Laura M.	106	1773	Lydia (Dudley),	34
1821	Larned H.	45	1834	Lydia E. (Geer),	59
1740	Leah (Benton),	14	1818	Lydia L. (Rogers),	45
1872	Lely L.	96	1796	Lydia M. (Rassequia),	44
	Lemuel,	32	1858	Lynn T.	96
	Lemuel,	49	1757	Mabel,	26
1830	Lemuel,	50	1878	Mabel E.	141
	Lemuel,	51		Mahala,	99
1883	Leon G.	120	1846	Margaret E.	79
1731	Levi,	14	1705	Margery (Collins),	31
1768	Levi,	21		Marenda (Emerson),	33
1833	Levi,	54	1799	Maria (Cruttenden),	31
	Levi,	99	1812	Maria (Mason),	45
	Levi,	100		Maria (Ellis),	50
1805	Lewis,	45		Maria,	46
	Lewis,	64	1824	Maria (Sault),	66
1844	Lewis B.	64		Maria,	98
1833	Lewis E.	113	1816	Maria A. (Maxon),	58
1866	Lillie M.	98	1867	Maria S.	116
1777	Linus,	36	1855	Marietta (Mowry),	71
1852	Lizzie,	95	1836	Marietta (Conklin),	75
1868	Lizzie,	112	1827	Marietta,	80
1876	Lizzie H.	140	1826	Martha (Hallstead),	57

Born.		Page.	Born.		Page.
1826	Martha (Hull),	83	1714	Mercy (Hubbard),	15
	Martha,	85	1875	Merrick A.	96
1856	Martha C. (Reynolds),	132	1757	Miles,	23
1827	Martha E. (DeForest),	63	1785	Mina (Carman).	34
1841	Martha E. (Parmelee),	77	1779	Miner,	30
1860	Martha M.	132	1813	Minerva	45
	Martha,	138	1777	Miranda,	30
1672	Mary (Hooker),	11	1814	Miranda C. (Parmelee),	43
1701	Mary (Eliot),	12	1856	Millicent H.	73
1705	Mary,	15	1880	Millicent R.	125
1778	Mary (Sweet),	26	1872	Minnie,	109
1767	Mary,	27	1864	Minnie E.	128
1798	Mary (Ludington),	30	1836	Miriam A.	63
1806	Mary,	40	1795	Morris A.	44
	Mary,	41	1878	Murray B.	135
1820	Mary (Barnhart),	45	1804	Myrta M. (Edes),	44
	Mary (Field),	62		Nancy,	35
	Mary (Ellsworth),	84	1834	Nancy M. (Bishop),	79
	Mary,	102	1813	Nancy U.	46
1868	Mary,	124	1769	Nathan,	33
1859	Mary,	95	1776	Nathaniel.	33
	Mary A.	41	1861	Nellie.	132
1824	Mary A. (Morley),	57		Nellie A.	98
1810	Mary A. (Bradley),	67	1863	Nelson,	95
1829	Mary A. (Nettleton),	71	1839	Nelson F.	81
1827	Mary A. (Leete),	77	1856	Nelson S.	126
	Mary A.	95		Nettie,	94
	Mary A.	100	1749	Noah,	20
	Mary A.	113	1770	Noah,	30
1828	Mary C. (Dickerman),	76	1784	Noah,	35
1858	Mary E. (Smith),	72	1870	Noel M.	96
1842	Mary E. (Higgins),	72	1829	Norman,	53
1854	Mary E.	85	1868	Norman E.	99
1851	Mary E.	89	1783	Olive,	34
1870	Mary E.	99	1823	Olive (Clark),	55
1850	Mary E. (Fitch),	104	1850	Oliver E.	71
1853	Mary E. (Penny).	109	1850	Ollie A.	117
1829	Mary E. (Otto).	113		Ophelia (Myo),	84
1811	Mary F. (Crampton),	42	1790	Orpha,	36
	Mary F.	60	1852	Orpha (Minor),	96
1878	Mary H.	122	1851	Orphia J.	106
1825	Mary J.	63	1790	Orrit,	34
	Mary J. (Stevens),	63	1844	Orton R.	71
1847	Mary J. (Ford),	73		Oswell,	62
1838	Mary J. (Ross),	75	1819	Parne (Hotchkiss),	69
	Mary J. (Barnhart),	83		Parnella (Greatrash),	36
1847	Mary J.	111	1681	Pelatiah,	10
1881	Mary J.	145	1713	Pelatiah,	19
1858	Mary J. (Stoughton),	121	1744	Pelatiah,	20
	Mary,	137	1773	Pelatiah,	30
1825	Mary L.	82	1815	Pelatiah W.	44
1837	Mary M.	59	1883	Percy R.	125
	Mason,	59	1818	Perry,	64
1810	Matheson W.	45	1790	Peter,	37
1822	Matilda (Moorhead),	46	1758	Pharez,	24
1848	Mattie J. (Woodhull),	111	1827	Phebe (Green),	53
1683	Mehitabel (Labore),	10		Philinda (Leonard),	49
1714	Mehitabel (Brewster),	13	1846	Philetta (Marsh),	91
1867	Melina E.	99	1818	Polly (Powers),	58
1688	Mercy (Hooker),	10	1806	Polly,	62

Born.		Page.	Born.		Page.
1718	Rachel (Stone),	15	1712	Sarah (Whitney),	18
	Rachel (Hoadley),	23	1751	Sarah,	23
	Rachel (Wynne),	27	1754	Sarah,	24
1780	Rachel (Goldsmith),	32	1776	Sarah,	26
1781	Rachel (Olney),	32	1755	Sarah,	26
1823	Rachel (Olney),	53		Sarah (Seaver),	32
1802	Rachel (Taylor),	62	1820	Sarah,	48
1838	Rachel A. (Cole),	72		Sarah,	49
1839	Rachel I.	75	1816	Sarah (Dudley),	55
1823	Ralph,	63	1833	Sarah (Hood),	63
1872	Ralph H.	112	1826	Sarah (Powers),	74
1761	Rebecca,	27		Sarah (Young),	85
1843	Rebecca M.	58	1854	Sarah,	95
1869	Rebecca M.	88	1837	Sarah A. (Camp),	71
1714	Reuben,	12	1852	Sarah A. (Ethridge),	91
1764	Reuben,	18	1852	Sarah A.	109
1785	Reuben,	33	1838	Sarah A. (Bradley),	113
1814	Reuben,	52	1832	Sarah E. (Gibbs),	82
	Reuben F.	48		Sarah E.	83
1739	Rhoda (Rogers),	19		Sarah E.	99
	Rhoda,	32		Sarah E. (Edwards).	101
1819	Rhoda (Kidder),	50	1838	Sarah J. (Alexander),	72
1826	Rhoda (Stone),	62	1858	Sarah L.	73
1836	Richard M.	79	1830	Sarah M. (Adams),	54
1805	Rodolphus,	62	1837	Sarah P. (Gauchet),	75
1838	Roger C.	79	1852	Sarah T.	111
1876	Roger W.	131	1871	Sarah T.	130
1708	Roland,	15	1813	Sarah W. (Benedict),	44
1863	Rosa L. (Thompson),	121	1841	Sarah W.	77
1827	Robert B.	62	1822	Sereno F.	46
1859	Robert C.	133		Sherman,	39
1871	Robert W.	120	1802	Sidney W.	43
1806	Roxana (Goodwin),	35	1833	Sidney W.	77
1843	Rufus B.	79	1753	Simeon,	20
1812	Rufus N.	43	1781	Simeon,	30
1819	Rufus T.	98	1792	Simeon,	39
1795	Russell,	35	1801	Simeon,	45
	Russell,	49	1840	Simeon,	54
	Ruth (Handy),	18	1812	Simeon A.	69
1740	Ruth (Hoadley),	23	1722	Solomon,	15
	Ruth,	33	1746	Solomon,	24
1785	Ruth (Stacey),	38	1810	Sophia (Benedict),	55
1790	Ruth (Cook),	39		Sophia,	59
1823	Ruth (Rose),	47	1828	Sophia,	66
1677	Samuel,	10	1802	Sophia M. (Whaley),	44
1726	Samuel,	16	1829	Sophronia (Hoyt),	57
1766	Samuel,	25	1831	Sophronia (Squire),	71
1787	Samuel,	38		Stephen,	17
1811	Samuel,	64	1738	Submit (Goodrich),	17
1810	Samuel H.	40		Submit,	25
1794	Samuel M.	40	1821	Susan,	46
1830	Samuel R.	66		Susan (Webber),	49
1828	Samuel T.	58	1829	Susan B. (Botsford),	66
1809	Samuel W.	42	1840	Susan M. (Church),	71
1755	Sally,	20		Susie (Grandy),	32
1781	Sally,	35	1724	Sybil (Stone),	16
	Salmon,	41		Sylvia (Thomas),	32
1677	Sarah (Marshall),	10	1819	Tapher (Willey),	53
1705	Sarah,	12	1825	Temperance P. (Weeeler),	66
1712	Sarah (Leete),	14	1819	Thaddeus M.	62

Born.		Page.	Born.		Page.
1838	Theodore,	60	1826	William,	52
1814	Theodore A.	43	1837	William,	58
1856	Theodore W.	79		William,	59
1749	Thomas,	24	1800	William,	62
	Thomas,	36	1846	William,	95
	Thomas,	58		William,	125
1787	Thomas H.	35		William,	125
1781	Thomas Jordan,	36	1846	William A.	71
1815	Thomas R.	64	1827	William A.	72
1739	Timothy,	23	1853	William A.	73
1803	Timothy,	45	1863	William A.	93
1827	Timothy,	54	1854	William A.	95
1837	Timothy,	83		William A.	100
	Timothy,	100	1862	William A.	105
1829	Timothy J.	63	1860	William B.	111
	Trumbull,	39	1870	William C.	90
	Ulysses G.	100	1870	William C.	136
1784	Uriah,	36	1811	William E.	63
	Uriah,	64	1833	William G.	31
1827	Ursula (Webster),	71	1828	William H.	70
1852	Wallace M.	93	1854	William H.	72
1874	Walter,	130		William H.	112
1793	Ward,	31	1828	William J.	48
1856	Warren R.	96	1826	William N.	58
1785	Wealthy,	30	1821	William P.	47
1808	Wealthy (Goodwin),	35	1864	William P.	32
1822	Weltha (Jackson),	57	1793	William S.	38
1839	Wilbur F.	81	1845	William S.	81
1872	Wilford H.	136	1867	William S.	130
	Willard,	138		William T.	147
1713	William, Gov.	5, 9	1854	William W.	79
1645	William,	9	1853	William W.	89
1671	William,	10	1856	Willis D.	85
1711	William,	15	1845	Wilson,	86
1760	William,	23		Winnie,	100
1783	William,	26	1883	Zaida,	140
	William,	36	1855	Zaida L. (White),	89
1818	William,	45	1813	Zibeah R. (Scranton),	65
	William,	49			

INDEX II.

NAMES OTHER THAN LEETE.

Abbey
Sarah, 110

Abell
Addison A. 148

Adams
Sachariah, 125
William, 99

Adkins
Chloe, 117

Alexander
Eddie F. 123
George H. 123
John, 123

Anderson
Albert, 126
John, 126
Mary, 126
William, 126

Ashton
Cynthia, 121

Atwater
Jeremiah, 76
Susan, 76

Atwood
Anna, 72

Ayers
Edna C. 57

Bailey
Phebe, 49

Baldwin
Elizabeth, 17

Ball
George H. 146
Henry O. 146
Phebe, 146

Barber
Elizabeth, 25
Thomas, 25

Barker
Samuel, 26

Barnhart
Charles, 86
Rev. Clinton, 86
Deloss, 86
Ella, 86
Emma, 86
Franklin, 86
Franklin, 186
Harriet, 136
Henry W. 85
Hiram, 136
Orren H. 86
William, 86

Barnum
James H. 96
Jennie E. 96
William, 96

Bates
Submit, 31

Beach
Nancy, 133

Beardsley
Sarah, 60

Beebe
Hattie, 102
Myron H. 102

Belden
Harriet S. 101

Benedict
Ashman, 101
Elias, 83
Gertrude E. R. 147
Lucy W. 83

Benton
Ammi, 21
Ann, 28
Chandler, 21
Clara M. 21
Edward, 21
James, 21
Jesse, 21
Mary, 74
Raphael W. 90
Rene, 21

Bishop
Achsah, 28
Betsey, 28
Burton W. 131
Daniel, 48
Dexter L. 131
Elisha C. 148
Enos, 28
Eva S. 148
Ezra S. 79
Grace S. 131
H. Jennette, 149
John, 28
Johnson, 28
Leete, 48
Lucy, 28
Sarah, 79
Walter G. 131

Blake
Adelia, 117
George M. 117
Jane A. 117
John R. 117
M. Luther, 117
Reuben, 117
Roswell, 117

Blakeslee
Charles, 117
Edward, 117
Julius, 117

Blatchley
Esther, 25
Joseph, 25

Bliss
Fidelia, 93

Blossom
Wealthy, 108

Boardman
Marcia A. 111

Bohanan
Dorothy, 98

Booth	Page.	*Burton*	Page.	*Chittenden*	Page.
Lovina,	109	Albert E,	103	Abigail,	62
Botsford		B. K,	103	Calvin,	38
Henry,	115	*Butler*		Mary,	9
Bowen		Sarah,	109	Miranda,	29
Benjamin L.	115	William,	80	William,	9
Edward M.	115	*Button*		William,	29
George C.	115	Abigail,	135	William,	38
James L.	115	*Byron*		*Church*	
Bradley		Madora A.	141	Antoinette,	136
Abraham,	16	*Cadwell*		E. G.	136
Almira,	65	Jemima,	37	Harrison H.	119
Benjamin,	65	*Caldwell*		*Clark*	
Charles W.	144	Alfred A.	86	Dr. Atherton,	129
Clarissa,	65	Robert,	86	Rev. Azariah,	103
George,	65	*Callahan.*		Cynthia,	116
Henry,	116	Hugh,	140	Harriet S.	129
Joseph,	65	Sarah,	140	Isabelle H.	129
Juliana,	65	*Camp.*		John C.	102
Juliet,	65	Carrie,	119	Louisa,	102
Mary Ann,	65	James,	119	Mary,	102
Samuel,	65	Lillie,	119	William,	102
Sarah,	29	Mary E.	119	*Coe*	
Brewster		Sherman E.	119	Sally,	71
Anna,	20	*Cannon*		*Cole*	
John,	20	LeGrand,	129	Charles E.	122
Briggs		Olivia M.	129	Clinton P.	122
Sarah A.	105	*Carl*		E. B.	122
Brockett		Elizabeth,	101	Flora M.	122
Patty,	134	*Carman*		Jennie M.	122
Brooks		John,	56	*Collins*	
Amos,	54	Joseph,	56	Ann,	12
Brown		Joseph G.	56	Anna,	22
Betsey,	36	Lydia,	56	Charles,	22
Bryan		*Case*		Charles H.	143
Sarah B.	124	Jesse,	38	Daniel,	12
Buell		Kelly,	38	Esther,	25
Emma A.	76	Mary,	42	Gurdon,	22
Jane E.	110	Sarah,	38	John,	11
Lucy,	80	Silas,	38	John,	12
Zephaniah,	76	*Cassidy*		John Thomas,	22
Bunnell		John,	54	Margery,	22
Alexander,	56	*Chapman*		Mary,	12
John T.	56	Catharine,	131	Mercy,	12
Myron L.	56	Edward F.	131	Oliver,	12
Ruth L.	56	Edward R.	131	Phebe,	57
Salmon,	56	Ethel,	131	Robert H.	143
Salmon B.	56	Samuel,	112	Samuel,	22
Theron B.	56	Theodore L.	131	Sarai,	22
Burbank		*Chew*		Thomas,	22
Sadie,	142	Jane,	69	Thomas,	143
Sophronia,	54			Thomas B.	143
				Rev. Timothy,	12
				Colwell	
				Catharine,	141
				Rev. G. T.	141

	Page.		Page.		Page.
Combs		Mercy,	33	Charles,	102
Charles,	94	Molly,	43	Chester,	56
Fanny,	94	Noah,	43	Elizur,	116
James,	94	Samuel,	19	Florilla F.	116
John,	94	Timothy,	48	Frank,	102
Martha,	94	*Cummings*		George A.	56
Polly,	94	S. E.	136	James,	55
Susan,	94	*Cutler*		James II.	56
William,	94	Mary,	76	John,	55
Cone		*Dagle*		Jonathan,	45
Hannah,	70	Susan E.	145	Mercy,	22
Cook		*Day*		Miles,	22
Amanda,	75	Charles,	42	Nathaniel,	62
Andrew,	70	Charles M.	42	Plyman,	102
Jared R.	70	Loring P.	42	Samuel,	36
John,	75	Myron,	42	Selah L.	116
Julia,	70	*Dean*		Willie,	102
Lucretia,	70	Minnie,	146	*Dunn*	
Lydia,	69	William R.	146	John,	80
Titus,	69	*DeForest*		Maria A.	135
Cooke		Charles,	111	Mary E.	80
E. Maud,	148	Clarence L.	111	*Edwards*	
Florence F.	148	David W.	111	William,	124
Virgil M.	148	Elizabeth,	111	*Eldridge*	
Virginia,	148	George M.	111	Clara L.	144
Cooley		John L.	111	*Elliot*	
Lois,	79	Mary A.	111	Harriet,	112
Coombs		Samuel N.	111	Reuben,	112
Betsey,	86	*Denison*		*Ellis*	
Conklin		Arthur,	97	Abby,	92
Alfred K.	126	Avery,	97	Charles,	92
David,	41	Cora,	97	James,	92
Fausta,	41	Inez M.	97	*Ellsworth*	
Irene R.	126	Lillie,	97	J.	137
Maron,	41	Simeon M.	97	Mary L.	137
Mary I.	126	*Dickerman*		*Emmons*	
Seraph,	41	William,	129	Allen A.	123
Coughlan		*Dickey*		Asahel F.	123
Mary,	125	Mary,	100	Egbert G.	123
Coville		*Doolittle*		George C.	123
Alice B.	147	Giles,	74	Hattie L.	123
James A.	147	Nancy A.	74	Rachel A.	123
Minnie I.	147	*Dowd*		*Ethridge*	
Crampton		Henry,	118	Anna K.	141
Russell,	76	Rufus,	118	John W.	141
William,	76	*Downs*		Lena,	141
Crane		William,	143	William H.	141
Mary E.	145	*Doyle*		*Fairchild*	
Cruttenden		Maria,	99	Grace,	112
Joseph,	33	*Dudley*		*Farmer*	
Leverett,	48	Abigail,	45	Elizabeth,	72
Lucy,	19	Betsey,	62	Martha,	74
Lydia,	19				

162

Faulkner
	Page.
Charles,	133
Christiana P.	133

Fenn
Benjamin,	11
Mary,	11

Fenner
Albert L.	104
Alexander H.	104
Bela,	104
Emma A.	104
Irving S.	104
Olive M.	104
Orlando,	104
Weltha J.	104
Willis N.	104

Field
Eliza,	108
Fanny M.	76
George,	108
George F.	108
John,	76
John P.	76
Martha J.	108
Mary,	108
Mary J.	76
Oswell W.	108
Philander,	76
Rodolphus,	108
Roxana,	128
William M.	76

Fitzgerald
Ellen E.	61
Richard,	61

Fleming
Rose A.	136

Foote
Clarissa L.	132
Jonathan,	132

Ford
Charles B.	124
George E.	124
Wallace E.	124

Foster
Charles H.	124
Edward W.	124
George E.	124
Ralph L.	124

Fowler
Abigail,	13
Abraham,	13
Bela,	47
Charlotte G.	148

	Page.
Electa,	65
Emeline G.	104
George,	75
James,	65
James W.	118
John E.	77
Josiah,	62
Reuben,	75
Rhoda,	62
Sally,	47
Statira J.	80
Thomas,	80
Zerviah,	46

Freeman
Alice,	125
Cynthia,	125
George,	125
William,	125

Frisbie
Julia A.	66
Mary,	30
Stephen,	66

Fuller
Elizabeth,	83
George,	97
Louisa C.	97

Furlow
Eber,	137
Martin,	137

Gauchet
Daniel B.	127
Edward A.	127
Frank H.	127
James A.	127
Lewis L.	127
Mary,	127
Peter A.	127

Geddes
D. H.	138

Gibbs
Deloss W.	136

Gifford
Cordelia,	137

Graves
Ambrose,	113
Mary Ann,	113

Green
Margaret A.	99
Mary,	94
Sarah,	94

Greer
Avery,	98

Griffing
	Page.
Arlette,	131

Haight
Emma J.	110

Hale
Roxa,	57

Hall
Emma E.	90
Mary A.	90
Mary J.	73
Moses W.	97
Samuel,	90
Samuel L.	90
Sarah,	90
Walter H.	90

Halleck
Fitz Greene,	18
Israel,	18

Hallstead
Jesse D.	105
Mary A.	105

Ham
Helena,	74

Hamilton
John,	144

Hampson
Harriet,	87

Hanchett
Lucy,	83

Hand
George E.	46
Hannah,	25
Hannah W.	46
Harriet E.	112
Henry H.	46
Ichabod,	46
Joseph,	25
Sidney N.	46
Theodore F.	46

Handy
Daniel,	28
Daniel P.	28
Harriet,	28
Joel,	28
Richard,	28
Polly,	28
Wealthy,	28

Harrison
Cordelia,	107
James,	107

	Page.		Page.		Page.
Harvey		*Hoadley*		*Hoyt*	
Caroline,	109	Jonathan,	35	C. L.	105
Harwood		Samuel,	33	Ella D.	105
Mary J.	108	*Holcomb*		Flora J.	105
Haskins		Medad,	77	*Hubbard*	
Lillie,	138	*Holden*		Betsey,	35
Haswell		Frauces A.	93	Daniel,	15
Joseph,	72	*Hood*		Jonathan,	24
Hawkes		Wm. C.	112	Mary.	15
Mary,	121	*Hooker*		*Hull*	
Hawley		Andrew,	16	Andrew J.	137
Polly,	53	Ann.	17	Andrew W.	110
Sarah L.	91	Anna,	16	Austin,	110
Haynes		Elizabeth,	16	Barbara,	110
Georgia,	114	Esther.	16	Cassius,	137
Hepburn		James.	17	Charles E.	149
Dr. James C.	90	Mary,	17	Elizabeth S.	110
Samuel D.	90	Mehitabel,	16	Ellen B.	110
Herrick		Mehitabel,	17	George A.	149
Anson L.	84	Mercy.	16	Maronette,	110
Cordelia,	84	Samuel,	16	Martha,	137
Emily,	84	Samuel,	17	Timothy,	137
Maria,	84	Sarah,	71	*Humphrey*	
Nehemiah,	84	Sybil,	16	Susan.	63
Hess		Thomas,	16	*Hurd*	
Solomon,	82	Sir William,	17	Caleb Leete,	24
Higgins		*Hopson*		Daniel,	24
Albert G.	122	Ann.	22	Dorothy,	24
Amy M.	122	Hannah,	22	*Hurlbut*	
Anna A.	122	John,	16	Albert,	128
Carrie M.	122	John,	22	Arthur S.	128
Eddie M.	122	Jordan,	22	Emma M.	128
Effie M.	122	Mary,	22	George B.	128
Frank L.	122	Nancy,	113	James,	128
Mary A.	122	Samuel,	22	Walter L.	128
Nathan P.	122	Sarah,	22	William R.	128
Nellie M.	122	William.	22	*Isbell*	
Prentice,	122	*Hotchkin*		Mary E.	116
William S.	122	George.	59	*Ives*	
Hill		Harriet,	59	Hannah,	64
Abraham G.	128	Joseph,	20	Mary,	63
Chloe,	71	Lydia,	20	Timothy,	63
Elizabeth.	45	*Hotchkiss*		*Jacobs*	
George,	37	Charles,	118	Washington,	143
Laura,	71	Eber S.	133	*Jackson*	
Lydia A.	128	Eliza	70	Harlow,	104
Orphana K.	134	Emogen.	118	*Jones*	
Rosetta,	128	Henry,	70	Festus,	85
Samuel B.	134	Joel,	118	Louisa,	85
		John,	118	*Jordan*	
Hinman		*Howd*		Elizabeth,	10
Garwood,	111	Josiah,	34	Thomas.	10

	Page.
Keller	
Mary W.	73
Kelly	
Mary,	25
Kelsey	
Abigail,	27
James,	118
Orphana,	134
Sylvia A.	118
Kelton	
Isadore A.	149
Kenerson	
Josiah,	100
Kennedy	
Cynthia,	83
Thomas,	83
Ketcham	
Amy,	60
Kidder	
Fanny,	93
Hamden,	93
Olivia,	93
Oscar,	93
King	
Charles,	101
Dwight.	101
Frank,	101
George,	101
Joseph,	101
Martha.	101
Mary,	101
Kingsley	
Polly,	59
Kirkham	
Bedad.	127
George A.	75
Julia,	75
Laura,	127
Sarah A.	75
Labore	
Dr. Anthony,	14
Mehitabel.	14
Ladd	
Minnie.	141
Lane	
Jacob,	143
Lay	
Martha H. W.	78
Steuben,	78
Leavitt	
Sarah,	98

	Page.
Lee	
Lillie M.	142
Wm. Henry,	126
Leonard	
Franklin,	92
Lewis	
Dr. ——,	149
Harriet,	68
Linsley	
Polly.	77
Lippit	
Charles,	105
Loomis	
Adeline,	81
Jabez,	81
Loper	
Daniel,	102
Lounsbury	
Ann E.	132
Luckey	
Emma,	135
Ludington	
Jude,	44
Martha,	61
Magoon	
Flora,	97
Mahaffy	
Mary A.	99
Mann	
Alpha,	28
Philip,	28
Marshall	
Dorothy,	13
Eliakim,	13
Mary,	13
Samuel,	13
Sarah,	13
Marston	
Agnes,	94
Elisha.	94
Frances,	94
Frederic,	94
Ida.	94
Jane,	94
Jennette,	94
Mason	
Aaron,	84
George,	87
John,	87
Julia,	87
Thomas M.	106

	Page.
Maynard	
Abigail,	113
Freelove,	65
Lucy Ann,	92
McCarthy	
Miss ——,	118
McCord	
Andrew,	87
Anna,	87
Eliza,	87
Hannah,	87
Joseph,	83
Nancy M.	87
Robert,	87
Simeon.	87
Susan M.	87
McKean	
Mr. ——,	21
McNeil	
Irene,	107
McNemor	
Jane,	25
Meacham	
Horatio.	68
Meigs	
Ezekiel,	32
Jane,	32
Merritt	
Betsey,	108
Miller	
Zibeah,	64
Mills	
Benjamin,	39
Casamelia,	39
Miner	
Eastman,	88
James,	88
Mary L.	142
Sarah W.	142
William H.	142
William W.	142
Moon	
Albert,	120
Estella M.	120
Lester A.	120
Moore	
James H.	67
Lucy,	63
Sarah M.	53

	Page.
Moorhead	
Adelle,	87
Clara L.	139
Elizabeth,	139
Emily,	87
Grace E.	139
Jane M.	87
J. C.	139
J R.	87
Maud E.	139
Robert,	87
Susan L.	87
Moran	
Joseph,	140
Zaida E.	140
Morgan	
Charlotte,	40
Mary,	40
Morley	
Butler,	104
Morse	
Charlotte,	126
Mary,	98
Mowry	
Franklin J.	120
George O.	120
Ida L.	120
John B.	120
Murden	
Isabella,	81
Munger	
Ruth,	76
Mye	
Carrie,	138
Charlie,	138
Harvey,	138
Mamie,	138
Neely	
Hannah,	46
Nettleton	
Bani,	118
Edwin,	118
James E.	119
Marion S.	119
Sarah E.	119
Newhall	
Clifford E.	115
George T.	115
Harriet A.	115
Ida I.	115
Julia A.	115
Theodore V.	115
Thomas W.	115

	Page.
Newman	
Francis,	9
Mary,	9
Norton	
Aaron,	131
Abigail,	79
Alice A.	134
Ana,	34
Anson M.	131
Arthur B.	131
Bessie,	134
Bethiah,	30
Calvin,	126
Charity,	29
Charles H.	134
Clara M.	135
Cornelia I.	126
Daniel,	29
Daniel,	34
Diantha,	111
Ellen A.	131
Ellsworth,	131
Fanny,	131
Fanny,	133
Fanny H.	131
Felix,	34
Giles,	34
Hannah,	24
Hannah,	36
Harry H.	111
Henry W.	134
Jennette B.	111
Jennie E.	131
Joel,	34
John,	134
John B.	134
Joseph,	135
Linus,	34
Lucinda,	43
Lucy A.	134
Mary E.	131
Mary E.	134
Medad,	34
Nellie,	134
Rufus,	43
Sarah E.	131
Thomas,	30
William H.	134
Zerviah,	30
Nott	
Polly,	35
Olmstead	
Mehitabel,	41
Olds	
Helen,	135

	Page.
Olney	
Abigail,	33
Betsey,	31
John,	97
Sarah,	142
Stephen,	50
Orcutt	
Ann M.	41
Salmon,	41
Otto	
Charles W.	144
Lizzie L.	144
Page	
Gilbert,	118
Joel,	75
Sarah,	75
Palen	
Cynthia,	103
Palmer	
Daniel,	75
Isaac,	80
Lucinda,	75
Merwin,	120
Park	
Amos,	131
Helen,	131
Parker	
Edward F.	123
Jennie M.	120
Martha A.	95
Parmelee	
Ann,	27
Anna,	28
Benjamin,	47
Betsey A.	77
Catharine W.	129
Dan	77
David.	47
David K.	47
Elizabeth M.	129
Hezekiah,	77
John,	27
Laura C.	129
Samuel S.	129
Samuel W.	47
Uriah N.	129
Payne	
Anna,	9
Rev. John,	9
Pease	
Sally,	62
Peck	
William A.	116

	Page.		Page.		Page.
Penny		*Rathburn*		Daniel L.	130
Robert L.	143	Amelia.	121	Dwight S.	130
Perkins		*Rawson*		Harriet,	130
Albert E.	143	Sophia E.	125	Harriet F.	130
				Miner P.	130
Pierce		*Raynor*		Nellie L.	130
Martha.	50	Hannah,	21	Noah,	29
Pierson		*Redfield*		Rhoda,	29
Heman	128	Parnel.	48	Sarah,	29
Orlestus C.	128	Ruth.	113	Sylvia A.	130
Pitkin		Theophilus,	20	Zenas,	87
Ellen J.	140	*Reed*		*Rose*	
James.	140	Daniel,	145	Alvan B.	89
				Anna M.	89
Pomroy		*Remington*		Elbertine E.	89
Cynthia A.	107	M. Hattie.	124	*Ross*	
Pope		*Remsen*		George E.	127
Rachel.	53	Polly	64	George L.	127
Rebecca.	53			Noah W.	127
Post		*Reynolds*		*Rossiter*	
Maria,	123	George F.	148	Abigail,	18
		George L.	148	Bryan,	18
Potter		*Rice*		Timothy,	18
Mary.	51	Joel.	109	*Rowe*	
Powers		Philander,	49	Susan T.	145
H. Freeman,	106	*Rich*		*Royce*	
John.	125	Matilda.	50	Carl.	93
Pratt		*Richards*		Florence.	93
David.	82	Zibeah.	64	*Russell*	
Harley.	82	*Richardson*		Eunice,	49
Harriet.	130	H. A.	121	Ida,	137
Norton.	82	Rhoda,	51	Thomas,	137
Otis.	82	Sally.	51	*Rutherford*	
Sarah.	82	*Robbins*		Sarah,	9
Sophia,	82	Chauncey,	132	*Salls*	
Prout		Chauncey W.	132	Calvin.	102
Hattie.	148	Edward L.	132	*Sanford*	
Pugh		Elizabeth P.	132	Huldah,	116
Ann,	91	John L.	132	Lucretia,	67
Quist		Martha M.	132	*Sault*	
Louisa,	147	*Roberts*		Thomas,	115
		Ann.	133	*Savage*	
Randall		*Robinson*		Ruth.	38
Clara.	92	Ruth.	37	*Saville*	
Ella.	92	*Rockwell*		Mehitabel,	20
Lewis W.	92	Joel L.	132	*Saxton*	
Ranney		Sarah E.	132	Minerva.	127
Betsey.	44	*Rogers*		*Sayre*	
David.	26	Abigail,	29	Almira.	57
Jeremiah.	26	Amanda.	29	*Scofield*	
Rebecca.	26	Clarissa I.	29	Nabby.	55
Reuben.	44	Cora A.	87		
Rhoda.	26				

	Page.
Scoville	
Esther M.	134
Scranton	
Anson C.	113
Elizabeth.	39
Russell,	113
Timothy.	39
Seaver	
Ebenezer,	51
Seward	
Asenath,	32
Elizabeth,	116
Samuel L.	116
Sheafe	
Joanna,	9
Shelly	
Clarissa.	76
John,	19
Lucy,	19
Mary,	19
Shubael,	19
Sherwin	
Chloe.	139
Rev. John C.	139
Shipman	
Achsah A.	121
Edward E.	121
Lydia,	72
Simmons	
Anna L.	106
Wallace,	106
Walter L.	106
Slawson	
Rachel A.	145
Smith	
Alice I.	146
Edward,	126
Effie J.	145
Emma S.	146
Freddie L.	146
Herbert F.	146
James E.	145
John,	36
Mary B.	145
Nellie I.	146
Perley S.	146
William	126
Snell	
Adam R.	52
Chester,	52
John,	52
Mary.	52
Phebe,	52

	Page.
Snow	
Sarah E.	130
Spear	
Helen,	121
Spencer	
Nancy,	129
Squire	
Phineas L.	119
Stacey	
Nymphias,	67
Stebbins	
Cyrus D.	133
Harriet L.	133
Stevens	
Alexander,	69
Amasa,	69
Andrew,	69
Asa,	69
David,	112
David R.	112
Henry,	142
J. Sylvester,	69
Lucy S.	69
Lois,	69
Sally M.	69
Simeon A.	69
William A.	69
Stockwell	
Emma,	119
Stone	
Abigail,	16
Abigail,	61
Andrew L.	24
Bela,	67
Caleb,	19
Charles M.	67
Clara J.	67
Ebenezer,	16
Ebenezer,	24
Edward G.	67
Elizabeth L.	67
Hannah,	14
Irene V.	110
Jerusha,	25
Julius,	110
Levi,	25
Nathaniel,	16
Noah,	24
Olive N.	110
Rachel,	24
Rhoda,	19
Samuel,	24
Samuel E.	67
Seth,	24

	Page.
Solomon,	67
Sophronia,	81
Stephen,	24
Tryphena,	55
William.	14
Rev. William,	24
Zipporah,	24
Story	
Sarah,	40
Stoughton	
J. C.	147
Struthers	
Agnes,	144
Helen,	144
John H.	144
Mary L.	144
William,	144
Strong	
Arthur,	138
Carlton,	138
Eliza A.	85
Ellen J.	137
Gabriel,	85
Gilbert,	138
Lewis,	138
Nettie,	138
Rachel,	22
Robert,	138
William,	138
Sullivan	
John D.	107
Sumner	
Darius,	85
Sally,	85
Sweet	
Mary,	40
William,	39
Tanner	
Alexander.	68
Tapher	
Thomas,	32
Taylor	
James,	108
Mary J.	108
Sarah,	81
Thomas	
Amelia,	74
Fanny,	50
John,	51
Lucy,	48
Stephen,	51
Zara,	48

	Page.		Page.		Page.
Thompson		*Walkley*		*Wilcox*	
Annette,	138	Edward L.	89	Charles E.	74
Maria,	106	Francis S.	89	Helen E.	128
Robert,	147	James M.	89	Hiram,	74
Thumb		Richard W.	89	Oziel,	70
Mary,	84	Warren,	88	Sarah L.	74
Nicholas,	84	*Ward*		Zina E.	128
Tracy		Catharine,	43	*Willard*	
Susan A.	118	Hannah,	31	Adah,	75
John,	118	Huldah,	44	Lydia,	76
Trowbridge		Mary,	101	*Willes*	
Ann,	11	Inelus,	31	Eliza,	135
John,	11	Thelus,	43	*Willey*	
Mary,	11	*Warner*		Caroline,	96
Mary E.	129	Mary,	118	Wellington,	96
Truby		*Watrous*		Worcester,	96
Giles.	37	Rebecca.	23	*Williams*	
Leah.	37	*Way*		Sarah M.	147
Truesdal		Sarah A.	90	*Williamson*	
Sarah,	68	*Webber*		Lucina,	96
Tucker		Benjamin,	92	Polly,	52
Sarah,	122	*Webster*		*Winsow*	
Turner		Charles	92	Naomi.	45
Ursula,	70	Daniel,	118	*Winters*	
Tyler		*Weed*		Mr. ———,	108
Abigail,	49	Harriet	83	*Woodbridge*	
Abigail,	80	*Whaley*		Rev. Ephraim,	11
Vesey		Cecilia,	82	Rev. John,	11
Benjamin,	52	Harriet,	82	Mercy,	11
Eliza,	52	Justin,	82	Rev. Thomas,	11
Gilman,	52	Maria,	82	*Woodford*	
Jane,	52	Myrta,	82	Emily,	68
John,	52	*Whedon*		*Woodhull*	
Nancy,	52	Lois,	80	Charles S.	144
Nelson,	52	*Wheeler*		*Woodruff*	
Samuel,	52	Newton.	115	Harvey,	101
Walter,	52	*White*		*Wright*	
William,	52	Alice G.	120	Martha,	78
Vorce		Charles H.	140	*Wyllis*	
Hiram	84	Mary C.	79	Mary,	17
LaFayette,	84	Rachel,	29		
William,	84	William,	79		
Wagner		*Wickham*			
Eleanor M.	139	Dimis,	54		
T. S.	139				

ERRATA.

Page 11, line 1, for 8 read 4.
" 35, " 6, " 1799 " 1779.
" 35, " 36, " 1868 " 1808.
" 58, " 28, " 1883 " 1833.
" 109, " 10, " (250) " (259.)
" 129, " 9, add J. B. L. m. Mary Smith, Sept. 24, 1884.
" 144, " 2, for (524) read (534.)

www.ingramcontent.com/pod-product-compliance
Lightning Source LLC
Chambersburg PA
CBHW020313170426
43202CB00008B/584